THE ILLUSTRATED HISTORY
of the
ELECTRIC GUITAR

Michael Heatley

THE ILLUSTRATED HISTORY
of the
ELECTRIC GUITAR

Michael Heatley

Merchant Book Company Ltd

Published in 2003 by
Merchant Book Company Ltd
P.O.Box 10, West Molesey, Surrey KT8 2QL

ISBN 1-904779-02-6

Printed and bound in Singapore

CONTENTS

INTRODUCTION

Though it was yet to be electrified, the guitar as we know it today was probably originated and developed by Spaniards in the Middle Ages. You can, if you wish, go further back than even that to Egypt and Ancient Greece whose name for this instrument, kithata, has a familiar ring.

These instruments may have been relatively crude, but there's every chance that, given a time machine, we'd recognise such prototype guitars for what they were. For many years, the major advances related to relatively simple matters such as the replacement of the Spanish guitar's gut (later nylon) strings with steel efforts.

All that, of course, changed when the guitar plugged in. Since the arrival of the Fender Broadcaster (later Telecaster) as the world's first production solid-body, all manner of different shapes,

sizes and sounds have been seen. And no matter who the player, their choice of guitar can make them sound very different: compare, for instance, the sound Mark Knopfler gets when playing his Fender Stratocaster on 'Sultans Of Swing' to the altogether more earthy tones of his Gibson Les Paul on 'Money For Nothing'. It's Knopfler each time, undoubtedly – but the sound is chalk and cheese.

This book charts the electric guitar's progress, from the experimental early years between the two world wars to the futuristic instruments at the cutting edge of today's technology. It includes comments from and about many of the instrument's most celebrated players – for the electric guitar market has always been personality-led. Fans who enjoyed the music and have grown up to emulate their idols often use the same equipment: as Cheap Trick's Rick Neilson said in 1992, with typical wit, "If Eddie Van Halen

INTRODUCTION

stated he played his guitar in a bathtub, 100,000 kids would probably jump in their bathtubs with their guitars."

It was thought that the advent of the polyphonic synthesiser in the 1980s would see the electric guitar superseded as the dominant sound and shape of rock. But that didn't happen, and as we strum and pick on in the current millennium it's a certain bet that the electric guitar, the most significant instrument of the 20th century, will retain its status.

Shadows legend Hank Marvin, for one, has no doubts. "There's something about a guitar that a synthesiser doesn't have. All right, I know you used to be able to get a keyboard you could sling around your neck like a guitar – Jean-Michel Jarre had one. But you can pose with a guitar as you wander round the stage, – and, with rock music, posing is part of the deal, isn't it?

"There's something that's much more organic, more exciting and dynamic seeing people wrench notes out of guitars, with all the grimaces and posturing, than someone's little fingers wandering around on a synth. The guitar has this mass appeal – there's a love affair between guitars and human beings I don't think we're going to see go now, somehow."

We hope we've succeeded in celebrating that love affair in words and pictures.

EARLY DAYS

Without the electric guitar, it's possible we'd still have been listening to big-band jazz today. The horn section reigned supreme, and it was impossible for any stringed instrument to compete with its volume. Not that guitars weren't playing their part in developing the music – even before World War I, Americans could purchase an instrument for a mere handful of dollars. But could this emergent voice be heard?

The first answer makers came up with was the resonator guitar. The idea was to put resonating metal discs into the body of the instrument, thereby increasing its volume. Eddie Durham, who played with the Jimmie Lunceford Big Band, had tried to overcome the competition by modifying his guitar – in his case with a metal pie plate! John Dopyera of the National String Instrument Corporation (whose guitars were usually metal-bodied) started manufacture in the late 1920s, while the Dobro brand name became almost generic for the kind of instrument, wooden-bodied with banjo-type resonators, which continues to be popular today with country, blues and roots musicians.

The advent of the valve amplifier in the 1920s offered new and different

▲ Resonator Dobro

possibilities. But how to connect the instrument to something that could amplify it? Pioneers like Les Paul, of whom much more later, tried anything from telephone microphones to the innards of cannibalised record players.

Engineer and innovator Lloyd Loar experimented with electrification as early as 1923, developing an electrostatic pickup that sensed vibrations in the soundboard of stringed instruments. But it was an innovation ahead of its time and his guitars incorporating these unconventional pickups (marketed under the Vivi-Tone name) were not successful in the marketplace.

The Gibson ES-150 is, by common consent, the grand-daddy of all electric guitars. Introduced in 1935 and endorsed by jazz player Charlie Christian whose post with Benny Goodman's band made him the highest-profile player around, it was the first real step in a journey that continues today. Christian, who had been introduced to the amplified guitar by Texas-born swing king Eddie Durham, found that electrification transformed his playing. No longer was the guitar a part of the rhythm section, it could, punch out lead solos that, on record, were sometimes mistaken for a saxophone. Chords took second place to single-string

▲ Gibson ES-150

phrases, fattened by the near-distorted sound available from the amplifier.

Gibson's advertising patter was seductive indeed. "You hold it, tune it and play it just as you would any guitar, and in appearance it is only slightly different. But strike the strings lightly and you have a tone that can be amplified to whatever volume you desire. Adjust the tone control and you change the tonal colour from a rich bass to a brilliant treble."

While Rickenbacker's horseshoe-shaped pickups had encircled the strings, Gibson's, designed by one Walter Fuller, had a single steel bar that directed the power of two magnets, bolted below the guitar's arched top, towards the strings. When one string was found to be louder than the rest, Gibson corrected it by simply cutting a notch underneath it in the protruding bar! Though it sounds crude by later standards, the ES-150 was indeed a pioneering concept matching old and new technology that established itself as the premier inter-war instrument.

At 77 dollars and 50 cents in 1935, the ES (for Electric Spanish) -150 was not within the range of every would-be guitar hero. The more so, considering that another 75 dollar investment would be needed to buy an amplifier, let alone the essential hard case at 13 dollars and 50 cents. Surprisingly, perhaps, sales of guitar pick-ups to add to already purchased

▲ Gibson Hawaiian Style

nstruments had been going on since 1931 but were relatively poor. This can be attributed to a combination of poor installation achieving substandard results and the understandable reluctance of owners to butcher their prized guitars to accommodate an as yet untested device.

The pick-up was the crucial ingredient which made the electric guitar concept fly, and the man attributed with pioneering the pickup as we know it today is the previously mentioned Walter Fuller. He joined Gibson in 1933, and soon afterwards the straight-bar pickup, known as the 'Charlie Christian', was introduced on a Gibson Hawaiian steel guitar. In simple terms, a pickup converts the vibrations made by the guitar's six strings into electrical impulses. The frequency

of these will correspond to the notes. The means by which this is done are usually tiny magnetic cylinders of metal known as polepieces.

Slightly ahead of the game was Adolph Rickenbacker, working out of California despite his Swiss appellation, who supplied parts to National guitars. He teamed up with their Paul Barth and George Beauchamp in 1931 to put into production a basic six-string instrument with a small circular solid-body. This was known as the 'frying pan' due to its shape. As the first production instrument with an electro-magnetic pick-up, designed by Barth and Beauchamp, it is now considered the true forerunner of the modern guitar.

▲ Rickenbacker Frying Pan

EARLY DAYS

Although the Frying Pan was already on the market, two successive patent examiners questioned whether the instrument was "operative." To prove that it was, Adolph Rickenbacker sent several guitarists to perform for them at the Patent Office in Washington, DC. After many performances and just as many delays, the patent was finally granted in 1937 – but precious time had been lost and other inventors had by now developed and marketed electric guitars of their own. Even so, Rickenbacker had made an impressive initial mark.

The Rickenbacker Model B electric guitar made in 1935 looks amazingly futuristic even now; made of Bakelite, the plastic material used to construct early radio sets, it was made using the advanced injection moulding process but abandoned when the Bakelite was found to expand with increased temperatures, resulting in disastrous results tuning-wise. Eldon Shambin of Bob Wills' Texas Playboys was, legend has it, not allowed to use his on stage because, in his boss's unenlightened words, "when I hire a guitar player I want him to look like a guitar player"!

Some more conventional arch-top electrics would be produced in the 1930s, but Rickenbacker only started to enjoy major-league success after Adolph sold the company in 1953: more of that later.

▲ Rickenbacker Model B Electric Guitar

Along with Charlie Christian, Thibodeaux 'T-Bone' Walker is claims to have a pre-dated Charlie Christian in obtaining his first electric guitar in 1935. "He was the next one to have it," he said in a Melody Maker interview long after his heyday, adding "I was out there for four or five years on my own before they all started playing amplified."

Whatever the truth, Walker was a keen player of early Gibsons, spreading the gospel to the likes of BB King and Chuck Berry who followed in his footsteps. When playing with Les Hite's band he used an ES-250, purchasing an ES-5 in the 1950s that had three P90 'soap-bar' pickups and played it for over a decade. Walker, whose standards included 'Mean Old World', 'T-Bone Shuffle' and 'Stormy Monday Blues', inspired many major players over the coming years and was the link between the solo blues of Robert Johnson and Charley Patton and the band-backed rhythm and blues we know today.

And so to Les Paul, born Lester Polfus in Wisconsin in 1915, whose experiments in the electric guitar between the wars would bear impressive fruit in the late 1940s and early 1950s. Not only was he

▲ Gibson ES-5

EARLY DAYS

credited with being the father of the solid-body guitar, but he also invented the multi-track tape recorder in his home studio– a prodigious achievement, if not strictly within the compass of this book.

Les played his first guitar at around the age of ten, having previously taken up the harmonica. Attempts to amplify his acoustic via his father's record player having come to grief through feedback problems, he filled the inside of his mail-order Sears Roebuck instrument with items of clothing and then, more permanently, plaster of Paris. This led him on a quest to find the ultimate solid body which ended with a piece of railway sleeper. His mother suggested Gene Autry (one of the popular singing cowboys of the day) was unlikely to be seen on the big screen with such an item while riding a horse!

A more practical breakthrough came in the early 1940s in the shape of 'The Log', an instrument which lived up to its name by being based around a piece of solid pine four inches by four inches thick, to which two home-made pickups had been screwed. The 'halves' of a guitar body and a neck were then attached, giving the impression of a through neck.

▲ Epiphone "Log"

▲ Fender Deluxe Amp

Not as effective as a railway sleeper, perhaps, but it did the job with considerably more style. 'The Log' was built for Paul by Epiphone, nowadays a subsidiary of Gibson but then a leading independent instrument manufacturer headed by Epi Stathopoulo. (Epiphone had enjoyed limited success of their own with the Electra Hawaiian guitar, noteworthy for having an amp and speaker built into its case.)

▲ Fender Princeton

Paul approached Gibson's parent company, CMI, with 'The Log' in 1949, but was turned away. The runaway success of Fender's Broadcaster/ Telecaster caused a rethink, however, and the word was put out to "find the kid with the broomstick" who, by then, had moved on from having established himself playing guitar with swing bands between the wars to becoming half of a successful pop act with wife Mary Ford. Paul's link with Gibson would survive many ups and downs and remains oday.

Many major players of the rock ra, notably Led Zeppelin's Jimmy Page, attribute their early interest n the guitar to hearing Les Paul – n Page's case, when Les was still backing Bing Crosby in the 1940s. "I heard feedback first from Les Paul, also vibratos and things," he confirmed to Guitar Player magazine in 1977. "I've got all the Capitol LPs. He's the father of it all, multi-tracking and everything else…if it hadn't been for him

▼ Vox AC30 Amp

EARLY DAYS

there wouldn't have been anything."

Amplifying the electric guitar didn't seem so much of a problem as making a usable instrument. The first vacuum tube had been

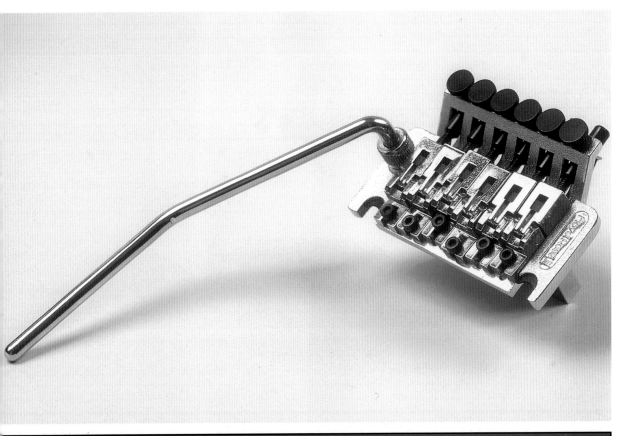

▲ Floyd Rose Tremolo

nvented by a man called John Fleming in 1904, the first amplifying valve for use in radios in 1907. Leo Fender and his partner Doc Kauffman manufactured around 1,000 combo amps (the term for a wooden chassis containing both amplifier and speaker) with an output of a princely four watts in the immediate post-war years for use with steel guitars in country bands.

By 1947, the first full year Fender 'went it alone', he had three combos with differing sizes of speaker: the Princeton (eight inch), Deluxe (10 inch) and Professional (15 inch). When a surplus of 10-inch speakers manifested itself, Fender invented the Dual Professional with a pair of smaller speakers, covered in the tweed cloth that would become a trademark. Come the early 1950s, Leo Fender's amps were as famous

EARLY DAYS

as his guitars.

In these early days, of course, the amplifier's sole purpose was to take and increase the weak signal generated by the strings via the pick-up and convert it to acoustical energy to be transmitted through speakers. No effects units or other changes to the source sound had been invented. It wouldn't be long, however, before tremolo effects were being offered as a built-in feature. (Tremolo is achieved by a small rise and fall in volume, as opposed to vibrato which indicates change in pitch: hence the often-quoted guitar 'tremolo arm' is actually a vibrato unit.)

Valve amps were the norm until the advent of the transistor in the 1960s which led to so-called solid state amps: these were much more powerful for their weight, but considered to be not as warm sound-wise by valve aficionados. The treble and bass tone controls of early amps would be superseded by sophisticated 'graphic equalisers' which enabled specific frequencies to be boosted or cut as a venue or required sound demanded.

Combos still existed but had been superseded for professional purposes by 'stacks' – a cabinet of, say, four 12-inch speakers fed by an amplifier sitting 'piggy-back' on the top. A 100-watt Marshall amplifier and a set of 'four by twelves' was a minimum for any self-

▲ Bigsby Travis Guitar

respecting rock guitarist of the 1960s. Prior to that, the set-up most to be desired was a toss-up between the British-built Vox AC30 and the Fender Bassman.

Today the name Bigsby will immediately bring connections with a purpose-built tremolo (or more accurately vibrato) system which is seen fitted to 'name' guitars. In terms of those systems, it is rivalled only by the Floyd Rose design of the 1980s. But Paul Bigsby, the man behind the device, also built guitars. And one in particular, the solid-body he built in 1938 for Merle Travis with the guitarist's assistance, may well have been the inspiration for the Stratocaster which arrived a decade and a half later. Ironically this did not feature a vibrato unit.

The 'Bigsby Travis' could never have been a production guitar, but while it remained a curiosity its through-neck construction, single Les Paul type cutaway and Strat-

like layout are all noteworthy. And while Leo Fender has claimed the headstock similarity was coincidence, Travis himself has no doubt his instrument influenced what was to follow. "I designed the Fender guitar," he told Guitar Player magazine in 1976. "Paul Bigsby built the first one."

If the inter-war years had seen many interesting one-offs, the post-war period would see mass-production come into its own. The secret of success was designing something that combined ease of production with the style of a hand-built instrument. Both Fender and Gibson had ideas up their sleeves, ready to go. The battle for the hearts, minds and dollars of a new musical generation was about to commence…

FENDER AND GIBSON

Discussion of the relative merits of Gibson and Fender guitars could take up a book in itself. Suffice to say that the two leading brands of electric instrument are almost mutually exclusive in terms of players identified with them. You're either a Fender man or a Gibson man…or, indeed, woman!

The biggest difference between the two was the fact that, while Gibson's early efforts had been based on amplifying the acoustic arch-top, Fender instruments had no pretensions to being anything but an electric guitar. Without amplification, they would not produce anything other than a muted whisper. It was probably for this reason that Fender diversified into amplifier design and building: a field Gibson entered but briefly. Fender amps are an industry standard today alongside the ubiquitous Marshall and are, as often as not, used by players of other makes of instrument.

The founder of the Gibson company, Orville H Gibson, died long before any electrification of the guitar was mooted. But by settling in Kalamazoo, Michigan in 1890, Orville (whose life began and ended in New York State) gave the

▲ Fender Broadcaster

company its traditional base.

He made musical instruments as a hobby while working as a clerk, his workshop measuring a very modest ten feet by 12 feet. The mandolins and guitars he produced were often unusual, featuring carved soundboards, black-painted surfaces, elaborate inlays and sides cut from a solid piece of wood (rather than, as was usual, thin strips). He would tear apart furniture to obtain the cedar, walnut and spruce needed to complete such quality instruments, the manufacture of which could take a month apiece.

In 1896 Gibson filed a patent relating to a mandolin with a carved top and back and solid sides. The bowl-back mandolins prevalent at that time did not, he said, possess "that degree of sensitive resonance and vibratory action necessary to produce the power and quality of tone and melody" found in his instruments. He also hollowed out the neck to create an additional sound chamber.

Orville's instruments would not be hurried: indeed, legend has it that a Boston company who wrote placing a large order were told that each would cost $100 and delivery would be completed "in 500 years." But in 1900 his outlook

▲ Gibson ES-175

FENDER AND GIBSON

appears to have changed when he met a group of businessmen who wanted to manufacture mandolins and guitars of his design under the protection of his patent. The Gibson Mandolin-Guitar Manufacturing Company was formed in 1902 with a capital of $12,000 and took over an old bakery as its workshop.

After 13 years had passed, the company had made such a success of things that it was worth ten times its original value. But Orville's health was failing and, on 21 August 1918, he died in Franklin County, New York. His sad demise would not, of course, prove the end of the story.

Musician and craftsman Lloyd Loar joined the payroll in 1920 and was responsible for the introduction of a number of innovative new instruments. His stay was short, however, as he left in 1924 – ironically in a dispute over amplified instruments. He would enter the field of electric guitars (as Vivi-Tone) rather sooner than the company he left. In 1944, Gibson was taken over by the Chicago Musical Instrument (CMI) company, setting the stage for many future developments in the electric guitar field. The arrival of former Wurlitzer organ supremo Ted McCarty two years later was also significant, paving the way

▲ Gibson ES-350

for the Les Paul and other solid-bodied classics to enter production.

But it would be the company founded by Clarence Leonidas 'Leo' Fender that would make the first mark in the field. He was born on 10 August 1909 on his parents' ranch between Fullerton and Anaheim, California. An interest in electronics first manifested itself in his teens after an uncle who ran an auto-electric shop sent him a package containing a storage battery and a lot of discarded electronic parts as a Christmas present. Leo visited his uncle in 1922 and a home-made radio displayed in front of his shop made a lasting impression. He began building and repairing radios at home for fellow students.

Leo graduated from High School in 1928 and studied to become an accountant, continuing his radio repair work at home. In 1932, an orchestra leader of his acquaintance asked him to build a PA (public address) system for him – the first of several he'd construct in the decade. And when Leo was made redundant, he went into radio repairs full-time. This then brought him into the world of guitars and amplifiers.

A one-off solid-bodied Spanish guitar fitted with a pickup from a steel guitar proved so

▲ Gibson ES-175 with Humbuckers

FENDER AND GIBSON

popular in 1944 that Fender rented it out to local Western swing bands. The huge demand he uncovered suggested he was on to something. After a false start with the K&F company (formed with Doc Kauffman, a former associate of Rickenbacker) the Fender Instrument Company came into being in early 1946. With 15 employees, a 3,600 square foot plant was soon needed; by 1953, they'd expanded to occupy 20,000 square feet.

Amazingly, Leo Fender could not play a single chord on the guitar, but there is no doubt that he knew what musicians wanted. And his first effort hit the target with ease. The Broadcaster, introduced in 1948, was in many ways a basic instrument – but it delivered. A solid guitar with one (later two) pickups, its maple neck was unceremoniously attached to the flat, uncontoured body with four retaining bolts and a plate, banjo-style, rather than being glued in. Though it wasn't apparent at the time, such details would set the standard for mass-produced electric guitars of all makes for decades to come.

Neither was there the option of a separate, glued-on fingerboard on early models, the metal frets being sunk directly into the maple. And while the truss rod, vital to stop the neck warping, was unusually inserted under the fingerboard during manufacture, the new instrument had its truss rod inserted

▲ Gibson Les-Paul

via the back of the neck, resulting in a contrasting walnut stripe inlay. Staying with the neck, instead of being angled sharply back to create string tension, the distinctively shaped headstock was flush with the neck and body – another simplification that worked.

The bridge and tailpiece, separate components on most guitars, were combined in a simple, pressed-steel unit that allowed the height and intonation (length) of the strings to be varied – though, with just three spring-loaded brass saddles for six strings, this was necessarily approximate. The strings themselves passed through the body en route to anchoring on the

other side by means of brass ferrules.

The result of Fender's work produced a sound quite different from the mellow tone offered by Gibson's semi-acoustic efforts. The Telecaster twang (the guitar's name was changed two years after introduction as the Gretsch company was using 'Broadkaster', with a k, on a drum kit) would become a staple of the rock musician's armoury. It was also a natural country tone. What was more, compared with the 'old school' of guitars, the sound would sustain forever.

Volume depended on exactly what you plugged the Tele into, but with no hollow body to contend with the problem of

▲ Fender Telecaster

FENDER AND GIBSON

▲ Fender Telecaster

feedback was almost non-existent. The twang was the thang, and Tele players could twang pretty much as loud as they wanted. As long, too: the first advertising copy extolled the virtue of a "thinner body which makes playing for long periods less tiring." The instrument it supplanted, in country music at least, was the electric lap steel guitar (not to be confused with the more complicated, pedal-operated pedal steel) which had prised open the door for amplified instruments in this notoriously conservative field.

For a cost of $189.50, the guitar player now had a spectrum of possibilities to choose from. The original three-way selector switch permitted use of the bridge pickup, neck pickup (centre position) or, when moved all the way towards the neck, the neck pickup whose large capacitor resulted in a boomy bass sound. This latter option would become less attractive with the arrival of the electric bass, and

> *"For a cost of $189.50, the guitar player now had a spectrum of possibilities to choose from."*

the mid 1950s saw the middle position changed to combine the pickups, the neck position activating the neck alone. With the original brass bridge giving way to steel, these were to be the major and only changes to the design for several decades.

It wouldn't take long for Gibson to respond. Ted McCarty, who became the company's president in 1950, had been keeping a watchful eye and decided "we've got to get into that business". And while the ES-175, which went on sale in

FENDER AND GIBSON

1949, the year after the Broadcaster, looked reassuringly traditional it was the company's first electric guitar to be designed as such from the outset. Known as a 'pressed top' instrument,

it pioneered the use of pressed maple laminate which would become standard on newer Gibson semis. Since it's still on catalogue today, it can be said (by virtue of the Broadcaster's transformation to Telecaster) to be the longest-running electric guitar in production. The more expensive ES-350 would be extensively used by Chuck Berry.

The ES-175's combination of single cutaway and P90 pickup was one other Gibsons would repeat. The

P90 (sometimes referred to as a 'soapbar' for visual reasons) was a halfway house between single-coil and humbucker, featuring adjustable polepieces and shallow but wide windings, and the result was a far more substantial sound than the Tele that was suitable for jazz and related music. (A double pickup version of the ES-175 emerged in 1953, while humbuckers would be offered from 1957). But the simplicity of the original design, with just a volume and tone knob, twin f-holes and Gibson's trademark back-angled headstock – to become a feature of the Les Paul in a few years' time – was attractive in itself.

Steve Howe of Yes is possibly the biggest-name user of the ES-175. He bought his

▲ Gibson Les Paul Junior

FENDER AND GIBSON

instrument in 1963 when still a beat-group hopeful with the Syndicats and continued using it up to and including Yes's early-1970s heyday. (His collection of varied instruments now runs to treble figures.) The ES-175, like Howe, has outlasted its flashier contemporaries and, with its combination of traditional f-holes and sharp single cutaway, remains a modest classic.

But Gibson had a bigger fish up its sleeve in the shape of the Les Paul, introduced in 1952 and a winner from the off that sold over 2,000 copies in its first full year on catalogue. Visually, it owed a lot more to its arch-top antecedents than the slabby Telecaster, its body (a combination of

mahogany with a maple top) being bigger, thicker and more dense. Its twin P90 pickups, selected via a toggle-style selector on the upper body and each with its own volume and tone control lower down, were also more powerful than the Tele's single-coils, the combination of bridge and neck offering a rounder tone. The fingerboard was the traditional rosewood, its edges were bound, and the neck to body joint was glued. The black, three-pegs-a-side headstock bore both the Gibson logo in mother of pearl and Les Paul's signature in gold.

The inventor of 'The Log' had certainly fallen on his feet. A five-year endorsement deal was concluded that Gibson hoped would win sizeable small-screen exposure for the

▲ Gibson Les Paul Custom

33

FENDER AND GIBSON

new instrument, Paul pocketing a five per cent royalty on its $210 asking price. And Les happily played along: the instrument that bore his name was, at first, only available in gaudy Gold Top finish, being the colour he himself had specified as looking best on television.

But, just as the colour choices widened, a whole family of Les Paul-branded guitars would emerge. Some, like the Junior, were intended as entry-level instruments to entice the novice (these cheaper versions, launched for those for whom a real Les Paul was beyond their price bracket, are covered in detail in chapter six) while the Custom, also introduced in 1954, was

considerably better appointed than its predecessor with gold fittings contrasting with a black finish. Its body was made totally of mahogany rather than being a maple/mahogany match.

As the Les Paul progressed, it moved ever further from its antecedents. The 'trapeze' style bridge and tailpiece was found lacking as the strings wrapped under rather than over the former to obtain a low action, making right-hand string damping all but impossible. This was soon replaced by a very functional stud-mounted bar (vibrato tailpieces are very rare on Les Pauls.) The P90 pickups it had shared with the archtops were replaced by humbuckers in 1957. The following year saw

▲ Gibson Les Paul Standard

34

▲ Fender Stratocaster

FENDER AND GIBSON

the standard Les Paul colour scheme change to sunburst, making the most of the guitar's carved, arched maple top, and this Les Paul – known, quite modestly, as the Standard – would become the definitive version of the instrument.

The humbucking pickup had been developed by Seth Lover in 1957 and was so-called because its two coils, mounted side-by-side were supposed to cancel out any unwanted noise by virtue of being wound in a different direction. The advantage of single-coils (as used in the Fender Telecaster and Stratocaster) is that they emphasise higher frequencies.

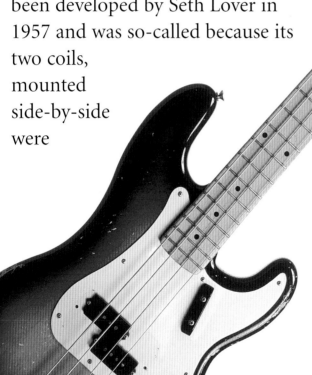

Original Gibson humbuckers bearing the PAF (Patent Applied For) inscription have become something of a holy grail for guitarists of a certain age and remain much sought-after. The patent was in fact granted in 1959 but the label carrying the three magic words remained until 1962.

Certain manufacturers like Alembic have since gone so far as to use a dummy pickup to cancel

▲ Fender Precision Bass

...um without losing frequency response, while Les Paul himself was in favour of 'piggy-backing' two coils one above the other which he claimed gave a cleaner sound. "But the younger generation wants distortion." And that was certainly the case for later Les Paul users, particularly those who followed Eric Clapton's lead in the late 1960s and onwards (see chapter five).

The divorce of Les Paul and Mary Ford in the early 1960s was nearly paralleled by a split with Gibson.

ironically, it seems to have stemmed from the makers opening a new building at the Kalamazoo facility that, at a stroke, doubled the size of the plant. This required new models to be introduced to ensure the extra capacity was used, and the instrument was radically redesigned to become what we now know as the SG (Standard Guitar) series. Les Paul and Mary Ford's hits had dried up in the mid 1950s, and the commercial advantages of having him advertise the guitar dwindled accordingly. What was more, with the guitarist and Gibson's contract coming up for renewal and divorce on the cards, it was deemed sensible to cease the connection in case it became part

▲ Fender Jazz Bass

of any settlement.

Paul's name appears on early SGs and, although he claimed he didn't like the angular design and sharp horns, one of these new guitars is actually pictured on an album of the period, 'Les Paul Now'. Even so, the period from 1964 to 1967 saw his name disappear from both Gibson's guitars and promotional literature. That was not, of course, to be the end of the instrument he'd christened…

Guitarists had only to wait another two years for Leo Fender's response to the Les Paul. This was the Stratocaster, a quantum leap from the 'Tele'

that would soon become the company's trademark guitar.

Even though Fender remains today one of the 'big two' when it comes to electric guitars, its reputation is based fairly and squarely on the first innovative years of existence. The Telecaster, Stratocaster and Precision and Jazz basses (the latter pair discussed in detail in chapter seven) are all still staples of the music world, and all exist in forms that would be immediately recognisable to players of the 1950s. Curious that such a supposedly revolutionary art-form as rock'n'roll should prove so conservative! It's also, of

▲ Gibson Super 400 CES

course, a tribute to the far-sightedness of Messrs Fender and Gibson whose pioneering work proved so close to the mark. And there's no doubt that, before they had had a chance to become accepted as 'tools of the trade', Fender instruments played a large part in carving a wild image for the new music.

It's very tempting to construct a time line that states: 1954 Fender Stratocaster, 1955

rock'n'roll. Yet a brief study of history will reveal the first records we now consider to be rock classics were fashioned

with older instruments. Elvis Presley sidemen Scotty Moore and Bill Black could, for all the world, have been jazz musicians, Black plunking along on an acoustic bass while Moore wielded a Gibson Super 400 CES, the company's top-of-the-range jazz guitar of that era. Sun stablemate Carl Perkins would also favour a semi-acoustic Gibson for some while. (Scotty Moore, incidentally, had bought a Fender on being demobbed from the services, but couldn't get on with it: "something to do with being a

▲ **Fender Duo-Sonic**

FENDER AND GIBSON

▲ Fender Music Master

feminine shape".)

With rock'n'roll taking off in 1956, there was a growing need for 'student' guitars of a size and price to appeal to new converts who liked what they heard and were anxious to join in. Fender developed a pair of 'three-quarter size' electric guitars in the Duo-Sonic and Musicmaster, distinguishable by the fact that one (guess which?) was blessed with two single-coil pickups.

Fender's ads extolled the virtue of a "guitar specially designed for old and young players with small fingers....provides all the playing qualities and design features every player needs." The bodies, however, were uncountoured slabs of wood, while the necks, at 22.5 inches, were a good 2.5 inches shorter than the standard Fenders to which the student could graduate when their skills and savings had grown. (24-inch scale versions introduced in 1964 were named the

Musicmaster II and Duo-Sonic II.)

Price-wise, the Musicmaster ($119.50) and Duo-Sonic ($149.50) were cheaper than the Telecaster ($199.50) and Strat ($274.50), but didn't wear quite as well. The anodised, gold-coloured surface of the pickguards tended to yield to repeated play, resulting in unsightly patches of the natural grey, and it was no surprise when these gave way to conventional plastic. As ever with guitars, however, pristine examples of these guitars now command silly prices. 'Alternative rock chick' Liz Phair confirmed their abiding attraction by posing with one for her eponymous 2003 album release.

The amps Fender intended these to be played through were combos combining both speaker and amplifier. They gloried in such names as Princeton and Champion (later shortened to Champ) and combos with those names are still available today. Not that eight-inch

FENDER AND GIBSON

▲ Fender Champion Amplifier

speakers would be described as 'heavy duty' any more! The emphasis was on bright, clean sounds, although it's ironic that these small amps are now known for their tendency to distort at the drop of a humbucker. It was the heavier-duty Bassman amplifier, with its 50-watt output and four ten-inch speakers originally intended to handle bass that would be used by the likes of guitarist Buddy Guy to cut through the noise of Chicago blues clubs, setting a precedent for the heavy rockers of the late 1960s to follow.

Gibson continued with their archtops, slimming down the body to create the Byrdland in 1955. Unusually for a guitar whose name design (by Billy Byrd and Hank Garland) suggests an affinity with jazz, the marque's most notorious user is heavy metal legend Ted Nugent. He was impressed when he saw Mitch Ryder in concert in his native Detroit and noticed guitarist Jimmy

McCarty was playing one. But semi-acoustics and heavy metal do not mix. "I was bent on playing loud, and to do that you either have to eliminate feedback by buying a different guitar – or learn to control it. I started putting the feedback to good use."

On the debit side, Nugent is an example of the physical price loud music from electric guitars can exact. "My left ear is gone," he told this author in 2001, but my right ear works fine. I've always worn an earplug in my right ear literally since 1963-64. Very smart to do that. Now just once a year I pick a show where I get to take my earplugs out completely and just suck it all up, 'cause there's

▲ Gibson Byrdland

"Leo Fender ran his company until 1965 when, after a bout of ill-health he sold it to CBS for a reported $13 million."

such an edge that I crave." Such damage, he claims, is "a small price to pay" - even though he has to wear amplifiers in his ears to pursue the other love of his life, hunting wild animals.

Other notable Gibson archtops to flourish without the patronage of the wildman of rock included the ES-5 Switchmaster which, like the Byrdland, would acquire humbucking pickups and styling changes over the years. But the major Gibson semi-acoustic would owe as much to the Les Paul as the archtop: the history of the ES-335 is discussed in the next chapter.

As previously mentioned, Orville Gibson had to look down from guitar heaven at the pioneering work of the company to which he gave his name. Leo Fender ran his company until 1965 when, after a bout of ill-health he sold it to CBS for a reported $13 million. Yet he would remain a legend. The Los Angeles Times reported that Rolling Stone Keith Richards accepted his induction into the Rock & Roll Hall of Fame in 1989 with this statement: "Thank God for Leo Fender, who makes these instruments for us to play."

Even Orville would surely say amen to that…

FENDER AND GIBSON

▲ Gibson ES-335

THE ROCKIN' ROLLIN' 1950s

Having set the industry standard with the Broadcaster / Telecaster, Fender offered a stunning development in 1954 with the Stratocaster. The 'Strat', as it's universally termed, is perhaps the quintessential rock guitar: certainly, no other has been imitated as often. Its revolutionary double cutaway format would become the pattern for other original designs too, having clear advantages in terms of both balance and access to the upper fretboard.

"Adding to the visual appeal, the jack socket was semi-recessed onto the body..."

Where the Broadcaster and Les Paul both offered two pickups, the Strat went one better. Not only that, it offered many different options thanks to a three-way selector switch that, guitarists quickly found, could be wedged between settings: hence, instead of just using neck, centre and bridge pickups at one time, you could have neck and centre or bridge and centre, allowing five different sounds to be obtained. The combined sounds were funky and out of phase, and can be heard in the playing of Eric Clapton, JJ Cale and Mark Knopfler.

The Strat's pickups were single-coil and mounted on the large scratchplate, as were the three knobs – a master volume plus tone for the neck and middle pickups (the bridge was assumed to be the brightest and therefore not requiring modification). Adding to the visual appeal, the jack socket was semi-recessed onto the body via a teardrop-shaped metal plate, meaning that less damage would be caused if the instrument should be dropped than if the plug entered the body in perpendicular fashion.

Its single-piece neck was reminiscent of the Telecaster and was attached to the body in an identical way. The headstock, though still flush with neck and body, was fuller and more rounded, almost exactly like the pre-war Bigsby Travis.

Perhaps the biggest innovation the Strat offered for its $249.50 pricetag was its so-called tremolo bridge, operated by a plastic-tipped metal bar. Strictly speaking it should be termed a vibrato unit, tremolo referring to changes in volume not pitch – but what the hell, the ability to use a 'whammy bar' would become one of the basic rock skills. And in the hands of the likes of Jimi Hendrix (see chapter five), it would help change the face of music.

Altering the six strings' pitch was made possible by passing them over a 'floating' bridge and anchoring them in a cavity at the back of the body. The necessary tension was provided by five springs, also in the cavity, though some guitarists would reduce their number to three. 'Hard-tail' Strats simply aped the Telecaster in having six brass retainers at the rear of

▲ Vega Guitar

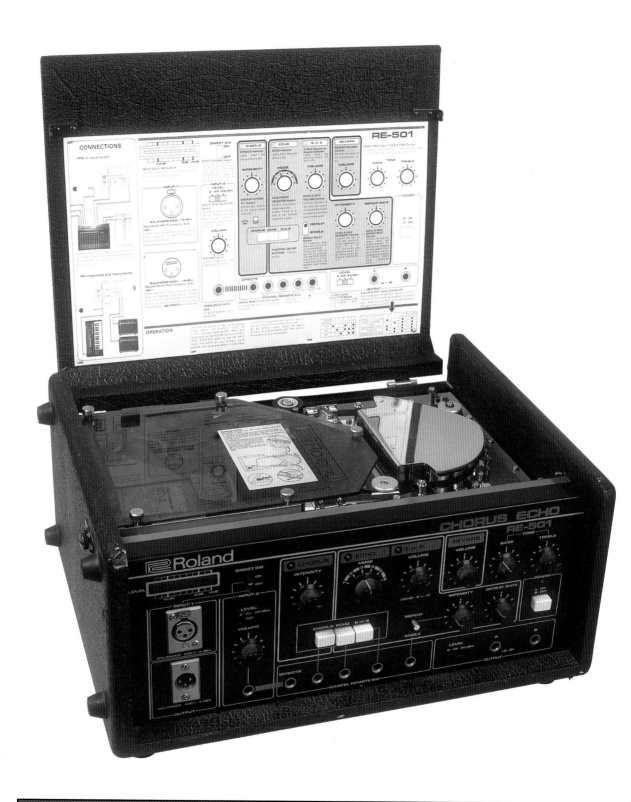

▲ Echoplex

THE ROCKIN' ROLLIN' 1950s

he body rather than the routed-out cavity with its plastic 'lid'.

Bespectacled, nerdish, Buddy Holly certainly wouldn't be thought of today as a typical guitar stylist, but there's little doubt that his album 'The Chirping Crickets', released in 1957, did more for Fender Stratocasters than any ad campaign ever could. Not only was the music on the vinyl truly stunning, the fact that he was pictured with his sunburst Strat on the sleeve made the connection crystal clear.

The Crickets were a self-contained outfit as happy on stage as in the studio who recorded self-penned songs without the need for outside assistance. Holly's guitar breaks owed much to his country and rockabilly heritage, but his lead playing was both brief and concise. Rhythmically, he has often been imitated but rarely equalled.

Sadly, of course Holly perished in a plane crash in 1959, 'the day the music died' as Don McLean so eloquently put it. In 2000, a re-enactment of the Winter Dance Party went on tour with John Mueller, a musician and actor, in the Holly role. He was accompanied by sometime Cricket Niki Sullivan and

▲ Gretsch Elector II Cutaway

JP Richardson Jr, the son of the Big Bopper (of 'Chantilly Lace' fame) who also perished. Interestingly Mueller not only used a 1957 Strat identical to Holly's one but also located heavy flatwound strings to make his recreation that little bit more accurate.

Holly was, sadly, history, but rock'n'roll, and the Strat, lived on. Gene Vincent's lead guitarist in the Blue Caps, Johnny Meeks, who took over from Cliff Gallup, would prove very influential on a generation of players, from Hank Marvin to Jeff Beck, exhibiting his piercing-toned Strat style on classic tracks like 'Summertime' and 'Dance To The Bop'.

The instrument changed little in its first half-decade – indeed, until the 1960s very few Strats were seen that were not sunburst finish (occasionally blond) and they invariably had a one-piece maple neck rather than the rosewood fingerboard adopted in 1959. The headstock would be enlarged in 1965 to counter problems with warping, but even then (and today) the basics remained unchanged.

The late 1950s blues sired its own brand of guitar heroes, many of whom would influence the musicians who created rock a decade latter. Buddy Guy and Otis Rush were

▲ Gretsch 6120

among notable Strat users. Guy adopted the instrument after seeing Guitar Slim "tearing 'em up…I wanted to be like him." While in Africa in 1969, his guitar case fell off the roof rack of his car and opened on the road: "It got scratched up, but only the E string was out of tune." Guy would be the reason Stevie Ray Vaughan, the leading white blues player of the 1980s, chose a Strat – testimony in itself to his influence.

Guy's high-volume combination of Stratocaster and Fender Bassman combo, with its four 10-inch speakers, would prove staggeringly influential. Interestingly, and unlike SRV, Guy never had his own signature guitar. When he selected the neck and appointments for one, Fender discovered his and Eric Clapton's taste were too similar to market separate instruments!

Like Albert King, Otis Rush's style was influenced by playing a

> *"Guy would be the reason Stevie Ray Vaughan, the leading white blues player of the 1980s, chose a Strat – testimony in itself to his influence."*

right-handed guitar upside-down, southpaw style. "I play the blues on the Strat," he's said, "but if I want to play Jimmy Smith stuff or Kenny Burrell chords, I use the Gibson." (Indeed, he was pictured on 1969's 'Mourning In The Morning' album cradling a Gibson-made Epiphone semi-acoustic.) By the 1990s, Rush had come full circle and was playing a replica of a 1962 Strat with Vintage Reissue pickups, proclaiming it "the best guitar I ever played."

In total contrast, Hank B Marvin (real name Brian Rankin) was Britain's first home-grown guitar hero. With respect to the likes of Joe Brown who had preceded him, it was Marvin's exposure as lead guitarist with Cliff Richard's backing group, the Shadows, that made him the role model for many. And to Marvin went the honour, in 1959, of owning the first Fender Stratocaster in the United Kingdom.

The instrument was actually bought for Hank by Cliff, as the guitarist couldn't afford the £120 it took to import it from far-off California. Having worked his way through Antoria and Vega to the heady heights of a Hofner Committee, he couldn't wait to get his hands on the Strat with tremolo arm, birds-eye maple neck and gold-plated hardware they saw in the brochure. "It arrived in this magnificent tweed flat case," he told John Tobler and Stuart Grundy for their Radio 1 series Guitar Greats, "with lovely plush red lining. It looked a real treat – it was flamingo pink. You didn't have to play it, you just had to hang it round your neck and the

▲ Gretsch 1955 "Chet Atkins" Hollow Body Model, with Non-Standard Control Layout and Bridge

THE ROCKIN' ROLLIN' 1950s

▲ A Double-Cutaway Country Gent From 1963 as Adopted by George Harrison

▲ A Single-Cutaway "Chet Atkins" Country Gentelman From 1961

audience would be totally impressed."

The first Shadows single to feature the aforementioned Strat was a vocal number, 'Saturday Dance' – but its failure to chart led them to revert to their instrumental group format. The original guitar, which Hank eventually gave back to Cliff, ended up in the possession of his fellow Shadows guitarist Bruce Welch. Ironically Marvin hadn't realised his idol James Burton, the fleet-fingered player who worked with Rick Nelson before switching to back Elvis Presley, actually played a Telecaster!

Hank Marvin was among the first British guitarists to use an effect, a Meazzi echo unit imported from Italy, which would become and remains today a staple part of his sound. It was based on an aluminium drum coated with ferric oxide (the material used on recording tape) and had heads to record, replay and erase. Briton Tom Watkins would come up with a similar

▲ Gretsch Tennessean

solution in the Copicat, which utilised a tape loop, while the American Echoplex was also popular. None of these, however, was built to withstand the rigours of the road. (Marvin's current unit is custom built by a company called Echoes From The Past.)

The Shadows were instrumental (pun intended) in the development of the influential Vox combo amplifiers, a staple of the scene for a decade from 1957 until Marshalls stole their thunder. The original compact design featured a 15-watt amp feeding a single speaker – the Vox AC (Amp Combo) 15. This was adequate for smaller venues, but as the Shadows and Cliff Richard grew hugely in popularity after his first hit, 'Move It', they found themselves in Town Halls where more power was needed. hence the AC30, essentially a double AC15, which is described in more detail elsewhere.

Without access to Fender and Gibsons and with only occasional TV exposure to their heroes 'in the flesh', British guitarists were stuck with the unenviable task of working out how they got the sounds they did. One of the 'trade secrets' that only became apparent through time was that US guitarists tended to use lighter gauge strings (a .008 gauge top string) that were easier to bend than the stiff .013s that were the norm in Britain. As

▲ Gretsch Duo Jet

Albert Lee explained to Mo Foster in his book 17 Watts, "Duane Eddy and Eddie Cochran told how players would buy a regular set of strings and an extra first or light banjo string, move them over one and throw away the bottom string, That opened up a whole new world for us."

One enterprising music-shop owner in California, Ernie Ball, caught on and started marketing his super-thin 'Slinky' sets that would quickly become an industry standard – but if it was any consolation to Albert Lee, his attempts to emulate the sting-bends he heard on record with heavy-gauge strings certainly improved his playing!

The instruments manufactured by Fred Gretsch provided the most radical alternative, both socially and visually, to the Gibson-Fender duopoly in the early days of rock'n'roll. There's always been a visually exciting angle to the range,

especially when toted by some of rock's earliest pioneers like Duane Eddy and Eddie Cochran. Gretsch played up to this by offering his guitars in a wider range of colours than his competitors.

Drums, banjos and mandolins had been Gretsch's first stock in trade, arch-top acoustics replacing banjos in the 1930s. Indeed, a guitar labelled 'Electromatic Spanish' appeared in the 1939 catalogue, but war put paid to its chances. Then a surge of post-war optimism saw Gretsch, whose products had until then mostly appeared under other people's trade names, enter the electric guitar field with a will.

The first postwar fruits came in 1951 in the shapes of the Electromatic and Electro II cutaway semi-acoustics, the Electromatic Spanish having finally made it to the shops in 1949. But piano tuner turned electric-guitar guru Jimmie Webster was about to help popularise the brand still further. It may be significant that the 6120, for most players the ultimate Gretsch model, owed much to input from Nashville guitar great Chet Atkins. He collaborated with Webster to create a classic, and his name would become as synonymous with the Gretsch as Les Paul was with Gibson.

Atkins was country and western's up and coming star, exhibiting a style of Travis picking learned from the same Merle Travis Bigsby had made that famous 1938 guitar for. He, like Les Paul, had made TV appearances and was playing on networked

radio, as well as being a regular on the Grand Ole Opry. The link with Gretsch would prove mutually beneficial. (He'd also ensure his guitar got onto the cover of most of his albums, while more publicity came from bluesman Bo Diddley, whose distinctive rectangular guitars were also built by Gretsch.)

In some respects, Gretsch was ahead of its competitors. The Synchro-Sonic bridge allowing for individual string intonation was on the market before Gibson's acclaimed Tune-O-Matic, while the Gretsch humbucking pickup, named the Filtertron and designed by Ray Butts, was developed before Gibson's PAF, even though

▲ Gretsch Original Hollow Body

The Rockin' Rollin' 1950s

both appeared simultaneously.

But enough of innovation: Fred Gretsch was peddling tradition. There was something undoubtedly kitsch about the Gretsch, with its steer-head inlay on the headstock and capital G 'brand' on the body. But that's proved attractive to players like Brian Setzer of the Stray Cats whose rockabilly revival stance of the late 1970s and early 1980s cried out for the flashiest yet most authentic instrument around.

Top of the line was the Gretsch White Falcon of 1955 that's most often seen today in the hands of players like Neil Young, Steve Stills and, more recently, the Cult's Billy

Duffy. But the man who put the Gretsch on the map was instrumental guru Duane Eddy. He bought a Gresch Chet Atkins in 1957 when still a teenager, his father countersigning the hire-purchase agreement, and went on to use it on a string of instrumental hits. His style was playing the tune on the instrument's bass strings, producer Lee Hazlewood employing evocative echo (obtained via a disused water tank!) to heighten the effect.

Chet Atkins' help and influence was recognised when in 1957 he was given his own Country Gentleman, named after a track he'd released. There was also the cheaper single pickup Tennessean (1958) together with the

▲ Gretsch Travelin' Wilbury's Signiture

original 1954 Hollow Body; a briefly available Solid Body did not meet with his approval. (The biggest collection of privately owned Gretsches today, just under 300, is owned by Canadian Randy Bachman.)

Gretsch also produced more successful solid-bodied instruments like the Duo-Jet, a vaguely Les Paul-shaped guitar which Gene Vincent's first guitarist Cliff Gallup had used to great effect on classics like 'Be-Bop-A-Lula'. George Harrison also played

▲ Gibson ES-335

one in the Beatles' early career before purchasing a double cutaway Country Gentleman in 1963. It was Gretsch's response to the Fender solid-bodies, and was interesting in featuring a plastic covering on the front for visual effect which was a carry-over

from Gretsch's history as a drum-maker. It was also a lot lighter than a Les Paul because of all the routing out of the inner body and the fact that it was made from separate pieces of mahogany.

Gretsch guitars didn't adapt well to volume production unlike, say, the Telecaster which had clearly been designed with the mass market in mind. Contrast, for instance, a Gretsch's carefully glued neck-to-body joint to that of the

▲ Gibson "Lucille" Signiture Model

...olt-on Tele. It wasn't ...nusual for ...rospective mid-...960s buyers to ...e faced

with a long wait, maybe up to a year – even though the earlier output of 50 instruments a week had been upped almost tenfold.

Fred Gretsch left the company that bore his name in 1971, but bought the business back from new owners Baldwin in 1985. By 1989, they were ready to restore some famous shapes to the market, though they could no longer use the Chet Atkins name. The instruments were now made in Japan but, according to aficionados, played even better than the vintage originals. Maybe the highest-profile user of a Gresch

solid-body today is AC/DC rhythm guitarist Malcolm Young, who got a double cutaway signature Solid in 1997.

"The 335's best-known exponent is bluesman BB King, whose favoured instrument, 'Lucille', became so famous Gibson elected to manufacture it as a signature model."

61

THE ROCKIN' ROLLIN' 1950s

One of the first products, however, was no reproduction but a guitar to celebrate the success of the Travelling Wilburys, the supergroup made up of famous Gretsch user George Harrison, Bob Dylan, Tom Petty, Jeff Lynne and Roy Orbison. Though cheaply made, these graphic-fronted pieces reflecting the album artwork quickly became collectors' items.

Gibson's early reputation had been built on hollow-bodied jazz guitars before the Les Paul had caused a lurch to the solid market. Their next idea was to combine the best of both worlds into a semi-acoustic guitar – revolutionary at the time of its design in 1957, even if it took one step back to move two steps forward.

The instrument in question was the ES-335, an instrument whose distinctive double-cutaway shape would become a familiar sight in the hands of players as stylistically diverse as John Lee Hooker, Moody Blue Justin Hayward and Ten Years After's Alvin Lee. That list gives a clue as to the ES-335's versatility, for it could shine just as brightly in any setting.

Yet perhaps due to its less than macho image the ES-335 has never been considered as collectable as a Les Paul (early examples reach only around a third of Les Paul prices). On the other hand it has remained in demand (and thus production

▲ Gibson Explorer

ever since its introduction in 1958. Experts have called it the ideal combination of Gibson's hollow-body history with their solid-body future. Either way, it's turned out rather more than just a compromise.

A hollow-bodied guitar offered a crispness of sound solids could not match, but in terms of sustain the Les Paul could not be beaten. Gibson president Ted McCarty figured that a solid block of maple running through the centre of the body along the line of the neck would be the key to improving this aspect. Even with the block, there was clearly a significant weight saving over the Les Paul, an instrument many players found too heavy to play all night. Bridge, tailpiece and pickup were all mounted on the block, offering solid-body sustain, while the rest of the body could amplify and add depth to the sound.

> *"A hollow-bodied guitar offered a crispness of sound solids could not match, but in terms of sustain the Les Paul could not be beaten."*

The ES-335 debuted a new bridge, dubbed the Tune-o-Matic (later applied to the Les Paul), which was mounted directly into the body and offered both intonation and height adjustment. Two humbucking pickups designed by Seth Lover each had their own tone controls, as with the Les Paul, plus a selector switch (unlike the

Paul, placed slightly clumsily where a strumming hand could easily knock it). The slim neck-to-body join, combined with the double cutaway, gave the 335 upper-fret access equal to the Stratocaster.

The 335's best-known exponent is bluesman BB King, whose favoured instrument, 'Lucille', became so famous Gibson elected to manufacture it as a signature model. He'd grown up on Gibsons, a famous picture of him playing at Memphis radio station WDIA (where he started his career as a DJ) showing him with an arch-top and a matching Gibson amp. Though inexpensive, the instrument was a clear advance on his first - a piece of wire stretched between two nails in a wall!

▲ Gibson Flying "V"

THE ROCKIN' ROLLIN' 1950s

Having rung the changes through the 1950s, playing an ES-5, Fender Broadcaster and Gibson Byrdland among others, King bought his first 335 in the year of its introduction, but it is the thinline ES-355, bought a year later, that is the model for the signature Lucille. Its major visual difference is the lack of f-holes. King's style, alternating vocals with 'answering' lead phrases, is now familiar to millions, while a link with Irish supergroup U2 in the late 1980s for the hit single 'When Love Comes To Town' took his music to a new generation..

Having successfully developed the 335, Gibson slightly blotted its copybook in commercial terms with its final creations of the decade, the Explorer and Flying V.

It's important to mention them here, given that they were incredibly futuristic designs to have emerged from what was effectively the electric guitar's first full decade. Yet it would only be in the 1960s that they were fully embraced by players, so that is where they will be described in detail.

BEAT BEAT BEAT

The impact made by rock'n'roll on post-war Britain cannot be overestimated. Yet, with national service hanging around long enough to ensnare Rolling Stone Bill Wyman, and food and clothing rationing a very recent memory, the wherewithal to buy an authentic Gibson, Gretsch or Fender guitar was beyond the means of nine hundred and ninety-nine out of a thousand teenagers.

The skiffle craze had not required expensive instruments, being a 'make do and mend' British alternative. But acoustic guitars and tea-chest basses would only satisfy for so long. Lonnie Donegan, the king of skiffle, had used a war surplus pilot's throat microphone as a rudimentary contact mic, strapping it to the front of his acoustic guitar. But even staid old Bill Haley had strapped on a semi-acoustic – so if you weren't switched on, you weren't happening!.

Framus, Eko, Kay and Hofner were familiar names to would-be British rock stars attempting to ascend the slippery slope from nylon-strung acoustic to 'name' American instruments. Economics dictated a half-way house, and these

▲ Framus Strato

European designs offered a respectable build quality and playability for a fraction of the price of the 'real thing'.

Framus was certainly not the first guitar-maker from Germany, but one of the most ubiquitous in the electric age. Founded by Fred Wilfer in 1946, the name being an acronym of FRAnconian MUSical instruments, there were some 300 employees on the payroll by 1955. A second factory was established in 1966. A series of Strato three-pickup designs in the 1960s were as derivative as their name suggests, but featured the ingenious Organ-tone swell-volume effect operated by a spring-loaded handle below the bridge.

In the 1970s, cheap Oriental copies forced a number of firms out of business, among them Framus. One of the last products before their 1975 demise was a Les Paul-styled guitar built to the specification of Dutch group Focus's guitarist Jan Akkerman. Fred Wilfer's consolation was to see youngest son, Hans Peter, make a new start in the business by establishing the Warwick firm in 1982 (see chapter seven).

Hofner guitars, also built in

▲ Hofner Galaxie

BEAT BEAT BEAT

Germany, were derivative in design, cheap to buy but often eminently playable – not so surprising when you consider much of their hardware was manufactured by the respected Schaller concern. They ranged in style from the Strat-inspired Galaxie, with roller tone controls under the individual pickups and a next to ineffective vibrato unit, to the Committee, with its elaborate birds-eye maple top. The Violin Bass, favoured by Paul McCartney and actually a copy of a Gibson design, is featured elsewhere.

One attractive but untrue guitar myth about Hofners was that the fine veneers used in their construction came from Pullman train carriages dismantled after the war. When the Japanese wave of keenly-priced 'classic copies' engulfed Europe in the 1970s, Hofner, founded in 1887, simply reverted to their pre-rock speciality, producing arch-top guitars for jazz players, also diversifying into the classical field. "In the 1950s and 1960s they were THE guitar until they lost out to the Americans," says British

▲ Hofner Commitee

electric guitar pioneer Bert Weedon, who says "you hardly ever see a Hofner with a warped neck."

Soon-to-be Shadow Hank Marvin had played a Hofner until he could afford to buy 'that' Strat. "I had a Congress with a half-inch action. Funnily enough, Gary Taylor who's played a lot of rhythm guitar on my solo albums, has still got his original Hofner Congress. It's interesting just to see it. Gordon Giltrap, who's done a book on Hofner guitars, brought one down to show me when I was recording one of my solo albums. He knew my first guitar was a Congress. It was interesting to see how small it looked. It didn't have as big a body as some of the other shallow-bodied guitars, it was relatively modest for its size."

Nostalgic as the concept may now seem, it was the lot of some of the biggest names in British pop and rock to battle the near-unplayable. Eric Clapton, for instance, part-exchanged his acoustic for a double-cutaway Kay with a thick neck and a high action (the technical term for the height of the strings above the fretboard). Despite its being "a bitch to play", he persevered. David Gilmour, soon to be of Pink Floyd, settled for a Hofner

▲ **Hofner Club 50**

69

BEAT BEAT BEAT

Club 60, which he obtained for the reasonable sum of £30 – some £70 less than 'Slowhand's dubious purchase!

The previously mentioned Bert Weedon was a role model for many in this period, thanks to both regular children's TV appearances and his ubiquitous Play In A Day guitar tutor book which gave many future stars a helping hand. He moved on from being an early Hofner endorsee – he believes Paul McCartney and John Lennon "started to play Hofners because papers like Melody Maker used to advertise 'Bert Weedon plays Hofner.'" He then transferred to Guild who, after he had enthused about their Starfire, offered to let him design his own signature model. "I was thrilled because that was the first American guitar named after a British guitar player."

The Beatles were prime movers in everything 1960s, and the guitar was no exception. George Harrison's first American guitar, a Gretsch Duo jet, had been bought second-hand from an American sailor berthing in his home town of Liverpool – and he later recalled that, when he took it back to the land of its birth and played it on

▲ Double Cutaway Kay

▲ Watkins Westminster Amplifier

television's Ed Sullivan Show, "Gretsch sold 20,000 guitars in a week. We should have had shares…" Even at that early stage in their glorious career, they'd come a long way from the Watkins Westminster amp they'd put a bass and two guitars through.

The roll call of American rock musicians who attribute their 'conversion' to seeing the Fab Four on the big screen in A Hard Day's

BEAT BEAT BEAT

Night is star-studded indeed. And George Harrison's adoption of the Rickenbacker 12-string guitar, as first heard on 1964's 'You Can't Do That', was to add a new sound and shape to the armoury of a generation.

John Lennon also used a Rickenbacker, albeit a three pickup, six-string solid-body 325. This had been bought in emulation of jazz great Toots Thielemans, whom he'd seen in Hamburg, and he would use this from 1963 to 1966. The Fabs' Ricky obsession had a touch of coals to Newcastle about it, as despite the Germanic name the guitars were manufactured in California. Paul McCartney would also adopt a Rickenbacker, in his case the 4001S bass, but not until later in the decade

Rickys (advertised as "the Beatle backer", with a picture of moptop John alongside the instrument) would provide the meat in the sandwich of numerous classic pop singles of the mid 1960s – many of the most notable, of course, coming from the Byrds. "George played his Rickenbacker 12-string in the actual song 'A Hard Day's Night', the solo,"

▲ Rickenbacker 12 String

recalls Byrd Jim (later Roger) McGuinn, "and after I saw the film I went right out and bought one."

If McGuinn places himself firmly in the Beatles fan club, his adoption of the 12-string also allowed him to replicate the sound of another Merseybeat group, the Searchers, whose early hits like 'Needles And Pins' and 'Don't Throw Your Love Away' provided template for the Byrds sound. he didn't realise however that the Searchers used two six-strings to achieve the effect. He did, however,

discover that use of compression gave him the sustain needed to obtain what he called the "jingle jangle" sound (after Dylan's 'Mr Tambourine Man' lyric).

No matter: McGuinn had a Ricky and he used it to telling effect. 'Mr Tambourine Man' was followed by 'Eight Miles High', a track that not only exploited the 12-string's ringing tone but also mixed in Indian raga influences.

The Beach Boys also employed the Rickenbacker, its mixture of unison and octave-tuned strings making it sound as if not one but two guitars were being played. Carl Wilson had a

▲ **Rickenbacker 325**

▲ **Hagstrom Guitars, Futurama/Goya**

signature model dedicated to him in 2000, two years after his death, a proportion of the proceeds going to the charitable Carl Wilson Foundation. His first electric guitar, rented while his parents were on vacation, had been bright green – a colour seldom seen.

The Who's Pete Townshend became a Rickenbacker user in 1965 when the churning introduction of 'I Can't Explain' helped put his band the Who on the map. It helped add body to his sound in a three-piece instrumental line-up. But its semi-acoustic construction proved very much less robust than solid-body Gibsons and Fenders when it came to withstanding his habit of destroying instruments at the end of a set. Interestingly, the Rickys he put to the sword invariably had f-holes rather than the trademark crescent shapes on models for the US market: this was a feature of guitars made for export.

Unlike most semi-acoustic instruments which featured top, back and sides of separate pieces of wood, the guitar's sound chamber was carved out of a solid block of maple (normally two glued pieces), a two-piece back being added later. Rickenbackers aren't as often seen

▲ **Vox Teardrop Guitar**

BEAT BEAT BEAT

today, but enjoyed an Indian summer in the late 1970s when adopted by Mod revivalists the Jam.

Dave Davies of the Kinks was one of the 1960s' earliest guitar heroes. His Neanderthal riffing on the group's first chart-topper 'You Really Got Me' has been credited by many as the prototype heavy-metal record, and inspired Eddie Van Halen, an icon two decades on, to cover the song instrumentally. Davies' influences included bluesman John Lee Hooker whose "raunchy, gritty guitar sound" attracted him. Although he was also a fan of the Shadows,

"every amp gave that pristine, clean sort of sound, which I was fed up with."

Davies's answer to the problem was direct and to the point. "I bought this cheap little 10-watt amplifier from a record shop and thought I'd cut (the speaker cone) all the way round with a razor blade. I didn't think it was going to work, plugged it in and it made this amazing sound, so I took a feed from the speakers and put it into my (Vox) AC30. That was simply borne out of frustration and experimentation."

Davies, who used his brother's white Telecaster for 'You Really Got Me' but historically prefers a

▲ **Vox Guitar Organ**

Gibson Les Paul, L-5S or Flying V, thought 'All Day And All Of The Night' "was a much heavier record, because when we went to make a follow-up single people were in awe of us, whereas (before) I thought I was a silly kid with a silly guitar sound that nobody was ever going to like. With 'All Day And All Of The Night' you can play it now and it really does sound very sexual." Though some historians have claimed Jimmy Page, then a session man, played a part in the Kinks' early singles, Davies assures your author it was all his own work!

If Fender combo amplifiers had ruled the roost in the early days of the electric guitar, then Britain was to make its greatest contribution in adding two illustrious names – Vox and Marshall - to the amplification hall of fame. Although also a manufacturer of instruments such as the highly visual Teardrop, Vox had begun life as amplification makers. And their AC30 would prove the benchmark among valve combo amps in the 1960s. Introduced in 1959 and developed from the earlier AC15, popularised by the Shadows, its distinctive diamond-shaped fabric covering the speakers would become such a characteristic sight in the following decade

▲ **Vox Phantom**

that the Counterfeit Stones, the UK's leading tribute band of the 1990s, covered their modern amps with the appropriate pattern for the period.

Two 12-inch heavy duty speakers were fed by 30 watts of power, and the result was ubiquitous indeed: Vox's press ad of the mid 1960s featured the Beatles, who'd used the equipment (including the T60 bass stack and amplifier, with two 15-inch speakers), but also made the point that more than 60 per cent of the country's leading bands used Vox amplification. The appearance may have been less modern than the Fender – especially the antiquated 'pointer' style knobs – but the result was a classic.

But just as 15 watts had proved insufficient for the Shads, so 30 watts was not to prove anywhere near adequate in the face of rampant Beatlemania – and as rock bands played ever larger venues, so the wattage would increase to 50 and then a 100 watts. Speaker cabs would soon standardise on the 4x12 pattern (four 12-inch speakers in a closed 'cab' or cabinet). Marshall, makers of industry-standard rock

▲ Burns Marvin

amplification since being adopted by Townshend, Clapton and Hendrix, have their products described in the next chapter.

The AC30's price-tag of £85 put it well beyond the means of most teenage hopefuls who tended to rely either on home-made gear or the likes of the Watkins Dominator, whose 17 watts pumped out through two 10-inch speakers cost a more manageable £38-10s-0d. Equipped with 'full compass tremolo' which operated on two of the four inputs, it was advertised rather hopefully at the time as "A top quality instrument designed for the professional who needs the best". Even so, it was more usual to see would-be beatsters utilising all four of the inputs for different instruments as they played their local village hall hoping a brush with fame would be just around the corner.

Gibson and Fender's domination of the electric guitar market brought responses from European manufacturers who came up with what were generally variations of the established theme – though the attempts at originality were well worth seeing.

Hagstrom in Sweden had begun guitar manufacture in the late 1950s but came into their own as

▲ Burns Bison

BEAT BEAT BEAT

beat opened up the market: as well as producing instruments under their own name, they made guitars for Britain (under the Futurama badge) and even the States (where they were known as Goya guitars). Jimi Hendrix Experience member Noel Redding used a Hagstrom eight-string bass for three tracks on the second album 'Axis: Bold As Love'. Jimi dabbled too, but when it came to six-strings contented himself with known quantities.

The most famous user of a Hagstrom six-string was Elvis Presley, who strummed a semi-acoustic Viking in the course of his 1968 comeback television special. It's doubtful Bryan Ferry plucked the sparkly, plastic-fronted P46 solid-body with its six selector switches in concert: it was, however, the instrument he was clutching in promotional pictures for the first Roxy Music album in 1972. Made some 14 years earlier, it probably looked better than it sounded. Shiny-suited Roxy copyists ABC would introduce the guitar to yet another generation in the 1980s, while an impressive web page now caters for Internet-savvy Hagstrom collectors.

The name of

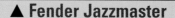

▲ Fender Jazzmaster

Vox is today associated with amplification, and their AC30 combo, very much a staple of the era, has already been described. But when they ventured into the guitar field they hit lucky with the Teardrop guitar which found favour with Rolling Stone Brian Jones, among others. (Ironically Vox guitars were manufactured in Dartford, home town of Messrs Jagger and Richards.)

The Stones' Bill Wyman was given a brand-new Vox bass – a signature model, no less – in 1965. "The trouble was they never approached me beforehand," he laments. "They just appeared with this awful, spoon-shaped thing and said, 'We want to call it the Bill Wyman Bass— we'll give you 5%.' I never did see any money from them – but then again I never liked their bass."

The Teardrop's visual appeal was obvious, but an attempt to offer a guitar with a keyboard sound in the Guitar Organ (with 18 – count 'em - knobs and switches on its body) proved markedly less successful. (Following the usual rule of 'unsuccessful then, valuable now', such instruments are these days worth ridiculous prices when in good condition).

Manufacture was transferred from

BEAT BEAT BEAT

Dartford to Italy in 1966, but Vox failed to see out the decade…and Bill Wyman never saw his royalties.

Teardrops and Phantoms, the latter a more angular variant available in six and 12-string versions and toted by Ian Curtis of Joy Division in the 1970s, are now highly collectable. The Phantom Special embodied an unique feature: an 'E' tone generator providing a reference for dressing-room tuning before the gig.

Another British manufacturer of the 1960s, Burns, were fortunate enough to hook up with Hank Marvin and the Shadows, still the last word as far as instrumental expertise was concerned on the British side of the water, at least. Having single-handedly promoted the Stratocaster into pole position as American guitar of choice, Hank now turned his colours – though in truth the Burns Marvin was very Strat-esque in terms of both looks and layout.

The story behind the switch is an interesting one, and was told to John Tobler and Stuart Grundy for their Radio 1 series Guitar Greats. It stemmed from a summer season in Blackpool where Hank, Bruce Welch and bassist Jet Harris

▲ Fender Jagstang

were all playing Fenders, "but Bruce's guitar seemed to be awfully difficult to tune. We had a couple of new necks put on but it seemed to make no difference. Then we were informed by the importers, Vox, that there was a problem with the positioning of the frets."

Welch having gone through 'literally a nervous breakdown" because of this, Hank contacted UK guitar maker Jimmy Burns 'with a view to seeing if he could make us guitars which would be the equivalent of the Stratocaster but would have a good fingerboard and be in tune." Hence the Burns Marvin came into being, with three 'Rez-o-Matik' pick-ups, a sophisticated vibrato and a distinctively scrolled headstock. Hank played his until 1970, when the theft of five guitars from the Shadows' van saw him reverting to his original Strat.

Burns would be bought by the Baldwin Piano and organ company in 1965, at which point its other main products were the Double Six (a 12-string guitar popular with the likes of the Searchers) and the angular Bison, also available as a bass. Various relaunches of the line have proved popular with 1990s groups like Oasis and Supergrass who have prized the instruments as much

▲ **Fender Mustang**

for their retro style as their undoubted playability.

An added bonus for Burns buyers is their colour options – among them eyecatching greens, blacks, reds and blues – together with elaborately decorated tortoiseshell pickguards which make other guitars look drab in comparison. The Korean-made Marquee was also popular as an alternative to the cheaper Strats on the market, though its origins were arguably a betrayal of Burns' 'handcrafted in Britain' heritage.

Having set the agenda in the 1950s for the next half century (though they didn't realise it at the time), both Gibson and Fender would have a very patchy decade. As suggested by the Hank Marvin anecdote above, quality control was not always of the highest order, but the problem – for Fender, at least – was improving upon 'perfection'.

The Jazzmaster had appeared in 1958 and, as the 1960s began, was heralded as "American's finest electric guitar", but its "unequalled design features and performance" didn't really add up to any great advance on what the Strat offered for the not inconsiderable price of $329.50. In retrospect, it

▲ Fender Bronco

probably did more in helping sire the Jazz Bass, its four-string counterpart, than anything it achieved in its own right.

Two huge pickups, giving a much warmer sound than the Strat and Tele, were intended to lure players of arch-top guitars, a field which was traditionally led by Gibson. The Jazzmaster was also the first Fender to offer a rosewood fingerboard, previous designs standardising on a pure maple neck: this, too, may have been an attempt to attract the conservative jazz market. Why, then, the angular lines of the offset body, and sliding switches for pre-set lead and rhythm

sounds? We will never know.

The Jaguar, introduced in 1962, was a close relation of the Jazzmaster but replaced the chunky pickups with Strat-like single coils. It offered a complex combination of pickup and tone circuitry which even owners found hard to figure out. Many players found it lacked the archetypal Fender attributes, especially as its 24-inch neck was an inch shorter than both the Strat and Tele.

The likes of the Beach Boys toted Jaguars, but it would have to wait until the 1970s until the Jaguar and

▲ **Fender Electric XII**

85

BEAT BEAT BEAT

Jazzmaster's anachronistic shapes became an asset in the hands of players like Elvis Costello and Tom Verlaine. Later still would come Kurt Cobain and his 'Jagstang' Jaguar/Mustang hybrid, but that's another story for another chapter.

Moving to the other end of the price range, the Mustang was developed from the venerable Duo-Sonic by adding a tremolo (vibrato) unit and whacking the price up accordingly. Though just as uncontoured as its trem-less counterpart, the Mustang, along with all its 'student' relations, would soon acquire a Strat-style contoured body. Medium-scale (24-inch neck) Mustangs predominated as, like the Musicmaster and Duo-Sonic, it was available in two length options. (The Bronco was added to the range in 1965, and was marketed with a matching practice amplifier.)

The period of 1963 and 1964 saw Fender move away from the sunburst and natural colour options to offer an ever greater range of 'custom colours'. These were often borrowed from popular automobile hues, even names like Candy Apple Red, Lake Placid

▲ Rickenbacker 360

86

▲ Fender Coronado

▲ Fenders 12 String Coronado

▲ Fender Marauder

Blue and Fiesta Red. Gibson soon followed suit, and the earliest examples of such hedonism – especially with quickly discontinued colours – now command big money prices.

The major Fender story of the decade came in 1965 as the company was sold to CBS – a company (full name Colombia Broadcasting System) whose logo had been more often seen on television or rotating at the centre of top-selling pop records. For guitarists, quality control concerns soon came into play: the perception was that instruments made under the aegis of such a large conglomerate could hardly match up to Fender's previous standards, so the term 'pre-CBS' has since been used to justify the premium prices of instruments made before the takeover date.

The first new design to reach the stores under the new management was the Electric XII, a response to the ubiquitous Rickenbacker 360 that never remotely reached the heights of its rival. Its Jaguar-esque body housed a pair of split-coil pickups, but the major recognition factor was a six-a-side headstock reminiscent of nothing else but a

▲ Gibson Double Cut SG

hockey stick. The Electric XII would bite the dust in 1969, though 12-string Strats have occasionally surfaced.

Another ill-fated idea of the era was the similarly offset-bodied Marauder, which with no visible pickups appeared to be the most unusual electric guitar of all. (They were concealed below the pickguard.) The Coronado ventured into Gibson semi-acoustic territory with a double cutaway F-hole design (a 12-string option was also available). This too failed to set the world alight. Fender's stock would, however, rise dramatically towards the end of the decade thanks to a man who, it is said, sold more Stratocasters than the whole of Fender's sales force combined. This was of course, Jimi Hendrix.

Gibson had, amazingly, dropped all connection with Les Paul in 1962, the last models to bear his name being re-branded as double-cut SGs, or solid guitars. But their first new design of the 1960s had been something very much out of the ordinary. The Firebird had been designed with posing in mind. The lack of an upper horn made the body look almost aerodynamic in its flowing

▲ **Gibson Firebird**

contours, while there had been a revolution at the headstock end of proceedings, too. The standard Gibson three-a-side tuning peg layout had been discarded in favour of an upside-down Fender profile, with banjo-style tuners that could not be seen from the front at all. This might have proved disconcerting at first, but players who persevered – like Johnny Winter, whose signature guitar it became – would soon be strongly identified with the model.

Unfortunately, Gibson considered the Firebird too similar in shape to its Jazzmaster and Jaguar and the threat of legal action led to a partial redesign. The result was the so-called 'non-reverse' shape introduced in 1965 which, ironically, introduced a Fender-esque 'right-way-up' headstock with conventional tuners. The 'non-reverse' Firebird also featured a glued neck as opposed to the original's through-neck design, the first Gibson to feature this. Unfortunately, despite Brian Jones' occasional patronage, the Firebird in both its forms would prove an endangered species, and by 1969 it and its Thunderbird bass counterpart had disappeared from the catalogue. (As ever, it would return as a combination of

▲ Gibson Firebird non-reverse

nostalgia and high prices for originals created a market.)

Even if import restrictions had been relaxed, there was no way every aspiring British beatster could afford a Gibson, Fender or Rickenbacker. The Watkins Rapier, first seen at the turn of the decade, was the first and best-known of their guitars, its name chiming in with the amplifiers (Dominator, etc) for which the company was best known. Though superficially an unsophisticated Strat copy, the Rapier was a part of the early arsenal of so many famous players that it

deserves a footnote in any book such as this. Respected session man Mo Foster wrote a truly excellent book, 17 Watts (Sanctuary), detailing his contemporaries' attempts to transcend their humble beginnings on instruments like the Rapier, and is well worth reading.

Cheap alternatives to name guitars were also available in the States, via companies like Danelectro. One of the mainstays of the range was the Sears Silvertone, made by Danelectro but badged for and sold by the giant Sears department store chain. With budget-conscious players in mind, Sears packaged it with a guitar case which featured a built-in speaker

▲ **Watkins Rapier**

and amplifier, the whole package retailing at a wallet-friendly $99.95. (Danelectro had been founded by one Nathan Daniel as an amplifier manufacturer shortly after the war.)

Danelectros were of deliberately cheap construction – their bodies weren't even made wholly of wood but utilised Masonite, a kind of hardboard – yet would prove favoured instruments with players for whom it was more important for instruments to "feel right" rather than what badge they wore. Silvertone versions of the Danelectro were initially distinguishable by having different shaped headstocks, but the Silvertone's 'Coke bottle' shape eventually became standard throughout.

Such cheap guitars lent themselves to risk-free modification, on the grounds of limited resale value. Randy California of US West Coast rockers Spirit 'hot-rodded' his axe, installing a theremin, while Jimmy Page (a major Spirit fan, incidentally) followed his example in the early days of Led Zeppelin. Page and California were both noted slide guitarists, and the bright tone of the cheap guitar favoured this. A feature of

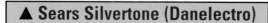

▲ Sears Silvertone (Danelectro)

BEAT BEAT BEAT

▼ Dan Electro Shorthorn

▲ Danelectro Longhorn

BEAT BEAT BEAT

▲ Danelectro Coral Electric Sitar

▲ Danelectro Guitarlin

Danelectros was their distinctive 'lipstick' pick-ups, their chrome covers reminiscent of the cosmetic in question, while the Longhorn and Shorthorn ranges with their exaggerated body styles were some of the era's most visually distinctive instruments.

Later in the decade Danelectro (who were bought out by the MCA company in 1967) ventured away from their cheap and cheerful beginnings into more exotic territory with the electric sitar. This was intended to capitalise on the era's appetite for Eastern sounds stimulated by the Beatles and was certainly easier to handle and use in the studio than 'the real thing'. "You don't have to be Hindu to play the Coral electric sitar!" ran a bizarre press ad, starring session man Vinnie Bell who had also masterminded the company's earlier Bellzouki 12-string. Another special was the 31-fret Guitarlin, a hybrid guitar and mandolin.

The first chapter of the Danelectro story ended in 1969 when new owners MCA cut their losses. A revived range of 'Dano' classics was offered for sale in the late 1990s, as well as

▲ Dan Electro Hodad

95

Beat Beat Beat

▼ Guild Starfire Bass

▲ Guild Starfire

▲ Guild Starfire

new designs such as the asymmetrical, Mosrite-inspired Hodad, but the revivals failed to sell in appreciable quantities.

Guild were another 'niche' American manufacturer to find a market in the 1960s, thought they'd started manufacturing instruments as long ago as the early part of the previous decade. They'd profited from the labour troubles of Epiphone, whose move to Philadelphia left the New York area rich in skilled guitar-makers looking for employment. Guild were known (and remain so) for their acoustic guitars, but by far

the best received of their rock-intended instruments was the semi-acoustic Starfire. It survived into the 1970s and has since been revived.

Guild's high build quality brought them the patronage of the likes of Muddy Waters, Jorma Kaukonen of Jefferson Airplane and the Lovin' Spoonful's Zal Yanovsky – not the biggest of names, but each with heaps of credibility.

Bluesman Buddy Guy was also targeted as an endorsee and briefly traded his beloved Strat for a Guild.

The Starfire bass proved popular with the likes of

▲ Guild S-100

BEAT BEAT BEAT

Chris Hillman (the Byrds) and Kaukonen's Airplane/Hot Tuna colleague Jack Casady. Other Guild electrics to find a market included the SG-alike S-100 (since adopted by Soundgarden's Kim Thayil) and the bizarrely shaped Thunderbird (no relation to the Gibson). Apart from its unconventional, asymmetric shape, this is memorable for having a stand built into the back – an innovation many players would like to have seen taken up by others. The asymmetric S-60D found few takers in the late 1970s/early 1980s but was a wonderful DiMarzio- equipped blues-rock guitar.

Having passed through other hands since going bust in 1988, Guild were bought up by Fender in 1995, who, as well as reissuing the Starfire and other classics have paralleled their use of the Squier name for cheaper instruments by reintroducing other designs under the DeArmond badge, the name coming from the pickups the company traditionally used.

The name of Epiphone is familiar to the young guitarists of today as the badge of Gibson's Oriental-manufactured

▲ **Guild Thunderbird**

budget guitars. Back in the 1960s it had rather more chutzpah, as evidenced by the fact that no less a group than the Beatles were enthusiastic users of their semi-acoustics.

Founded by Turkish emigrant Epi Stathopoulo, who arrived in the States in 1903, the company had been inherited by his two brothers on his death in 1943. But a labour dispute in the early 1950s led to problems and, on the death of another Stathopoulo brother in 1957, the survivor sold out lock stock and barrel to Gibson.

The company's capital E trademark echoed the Gretsch 'brand', and like Gretsch the Epiphone stock in trade was the semi-acoustic. While solid-bodies like the Crestwood found limited acceptance, being perceived at the time as 'poor man's SGs' (they are now, needless to say, collectable) the Sheraton and Casino were very highly regarded. The latter was owned by all three guitar-playing Beatles, and the publicity that surrounded their final live hurrah in 1966 before they retired to the studio to contemplate 'Sgt Pepper' saw the Epiphone image beamed far and

▲ **Epiphone Crestwood**

wide.

But when Norlin bought Gibson in 1969, the badge was transferred to Japanese-made copy guitars until the late 1980s/early 1990s when Epiphone again began to play a proud but still subordinate role to its big brother Gibson. The likes of Oasis's Noel Gallagher and Jefferson Airplane/Hot Tuna's Jack Casady have both been recent endorsees.

Rather as with Burns and the Shadows, the American Mosrite company decided to sign up a whole group to publicise their wares. And who better to go with than America's Shadows equivalent, the Ventures? The Mosrite Ventures model, like the majority of their 1960s output, combined a 'reverse' Stratocaster shape, with the lower horn bigger than the upper, two soapbar-style pickups and an extended three-pegs-a-side headstock with an M shape cut into it.

This popularity by association soon had the company, founded by Semie Moseley and Ray Boatright, multiplying monthly production tenfold to some 300

▲ **Epiphone Sheraton**

BEAT BEAT BEAT

guitars. The Ventures had always been particularly popular in Japan, so Mosrite reversed the usual flow of instruments by exporting many examples to the Far East. But just as more wild and sophisticated rock sounds pushed the Ventures out of the spotlight – in the West, at least – so Mosrite's appeal diminished and the factory doors slammed shut for the last time late in the decade.

But the guitar's reputation as a reliable honest workhorse combined with the utilitarian qualities that would see Fender's entry-level Broncos, Mustangs and Duo-Sonics find a new audience, led to punk musicians like the Ramones' Johnny Ramone adopting them. He bought his first at Manhattan's best-known guitar emporium, Manny's, in January 1974 for a more than reasonable $50, indicating the brand's unpopularity among 'real' guitar players at that point.

Semie Moseley re-entered the business on a smaller scale, and made Venture Don Wilson a special example with a fingerboard inlaid with his name in 1989. The group's

▲ Epiphone Casino

BEAT BEAT BEAT

Bob Bogle recalls that, though they never sold Mosrites from the stage as myth has suggested, they would often sell their equipment to a local group after a foreign tour "to avoid being overweight and bringing them back through customs." A nice little earner...

Ironically, Mosrite's production line shifted to

Japan after Semie Moseley's death in 1992, Johnny Ramone and Venture Nokie Edwards both receiving well deserved 'signature model' accolades.

It's clear, as we look back at musical history from

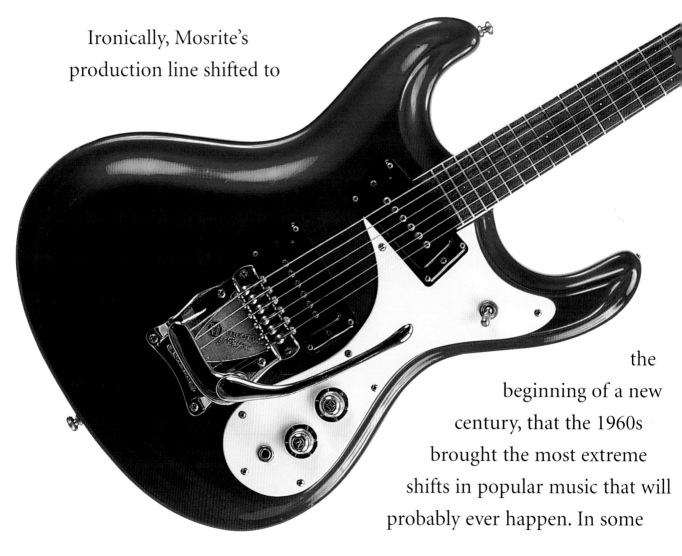

the beginning of a new century, that the 1960s brought the most extreme shifts in popular music that will probably ever happen. In some

▲ **Mosrite Ventures Model**

respects, the advances in guitar design and technology failed to keep pace with the musical innovation on offer – but then instruments are only a means to an end. The many different shapes and configurations that prospered but briefly are perhaps the equivalent of one-hit wonders – but, like rare records that are worth their weight in gold, are well worth remarking upon and remembering.

As we shall see in the next chapter, the late 1960s saw the return to production of the classic Les Paul: a case of one step back to take two steps forward.

> *"The many different shapes and configurations that prospered but briefly are perhaps the equivalent of one-hit wonders – but, like rare records that are worth their weight in gold..."*

ROCK REARS ITS HEAD

Progressive rock grew from blues roots in the late 1960s as musicians explored the possibilities of producing music to fill 20-minute vinyl album sides rather than three-minute singles. Pop and rock were diverging, the progressive route all about pushing the envelope and expanding boundaries. Classical and jazz themes added grist to the musical mill.

Cream were the first progressive superstars, the trio of Eric Clapton, Jack Bruce and Ginger Baker fighting for room to exhibit their musicianship and sometimes each soloing through a song. Clapton had first met Bruce in the ranks of John Mayall's Bluesbreakers, an outfit that proved to be the second finishing school for great guitarists after the Yardbirds (which Clapton had also graced).

It was the album 'Bluesbreakers With Eric Clapton', consigned to tape in April 1966, that not only put Clapton on the map with a vengeance but also led to the reappearance of a familiar guitar – the Gibson Les Paul. More than that, it inspired a whole generation of would-be guitarists to cast aside a conventional career path and 'go for it'.

▲ Gibson Les Paul Gold Top

The Paul's absence from the Gibson catalogue had in some ways been compensated for by the arrival of the SG, whose early examples had even borne the great man's name. But the less substantial body and thus inferior sustain didn't satisfy everyone. The absence of the original single-cutaway guitars from the shops led to a brisk trade in cheaper Japanese-manufactured 'copies', a situation that would continue for reasons of affordability even after the instrument was reinstated in production by Gibson in 1968.

Les Paul convert Clapton had been brought up on blues music: indeed, when R&B 'godfather' Mayall took him on, Eric briefly lodged at Mayall's home and was allowed the run of his record collection. Fortunately enough, many blues guitarists made a point

"Cream were the first progressive superstars, the trio of Eric Clapton, Jack Bruce and Ginger Baker fighting for room to exhibit their musicianship..."

of being pictured with their instruments, and when Clapton (who'd used a Telecaster with previous employers the Yardbirds) saw Freddie King posing with a Gibson Les Paul Gold Top he hunted high and low until he found a similar instrument.

"But Eric was the blues and it was a great relationship that was captured really well on that album."

Clapton played his find through a Marshall 50-watt combo, overdriving it to the point where a rich distortion was obtained. This caused several problems for the engineer of the 'Bluesbreakers' session, Gus Dudgeon (soon to be famous for his work with David Bowie and Elton John) as the guitar sound leaked into other microphones. But it was exactly what Clapton wanted. Drummer Hughie Flint believes this was the guitarist's secret. "We all really played down, whereas Eric was the only one who managed to stick to his guns and play with distortion and so on: we all toned it down, and it shows if you listen to it. There's some live tapes from the Flamingo – it's the same band except Jack Bruce is on bass– and on those tracks you hear how wild the band was. But on the studio album it's only Eric that really cuts through."

As has already been hinted, the album's impact was such that it's since been cited by a generation of guitarists from Brian May to Eddie Van Halen as the recording that inspired them to take up their instrument or devote themselves to it more zealously. Yet, for Clapton, it had been "Just a record of what we'd been doing every night in the clubs, but with a few contrived riffs we made up as afterthoughts. It wasn't until I realised the album was turning people on that I began to look at it differently." Gary Moore was one of the 'turned-on' youngsters and, aside from his numerous blues-related recordings, later showed his devotion by understudying his hero in BBM, the 1994 'ersatz Cream' with Jack Bruce and Ginger Baker.

Looking back, bandleader Mayall himself still rates 'Bluesbreakers' "a very special album. It was the first band where I'd found a soulmate, somebody who actually knew something about the blues apart from people who were just salient to it. But Eric was the blues and it was a great relationship that was captured really well on that album. It really stands up today musically. I can always listen to it."

A Cream-bound Clapton was succeeded in the Bluesbreakers by Peter Green for 1967's 'A Hard Road'. And though that couldn't possibly emulate its predecessor for breadth of impact, it had an equally profound effect in uniting Green with John McVie and Mick Fleetwood, the three musicians who would form the nucleus of Fleetwood Mac later

▲ **Gibson Les Paul Sunburst**

▲ Orange Amplifier

that year.

Green also played a Les Paul through a 50-watt Marshall combo, but eschewed the overdriven Clapton sound for a clearer, ringing tone. By some happy accident, his 1959 sunburst example had its neck pickup reinstalled wrongly, resulting in an almost nasal, 'out of phase' sound that quickly became a trademark when both pickups were used at once. The distinctive-sounding guitar, which he later sold to Gary Moore, was used on several Fleetwood Mac classics. 'Need Your Love So Bad', a chart single in 1968, is just one.

Interestingly, when Green returned to full-time music in

1996 with the Splinter Group, he didn't seem to have a trademark guitar any more. I asked him if that had lost its fascination after he gave up playing. "When you saw me in the Sixties it was always with the Les Paul. Any guitarist who has any success is going to try one. I used to be a one-guitar man like you want your heroes to be; it's in there with the music and the lyrics. If they change guitar, it changes everything for you – Buddy Guy, I'm thinking of. Rory Gallagher was like that too, he just had the one Stratocaster." Peter now uses mainly Strats, resorting to a Gibson Howard Roberts Fusion when he wants a fatter sound "for the Freddie King stuff".

With Clapton and Green the standard bearers, the Les Paul was back in fashion with a vengeance, other players carrying it like a

> ## *"With Clapton and Green the standard bearers, the Les Paul was back in fashion with a vengeance, other players carrying it like a sword in battle..."*

sword in battle include Jimmy Page of Led Zeppelin and Paul Kossoff of Free. The instrument lacked the Strat's familiar tremolo arm, the 'get out of jail' card for many a lesser player. But in the hands of Kossoff, whose finger vibrato was his trademark, that simply wasn't

> ## "Marshall was originally a drum teacher who opened his own musical instrument shop in London in 1960. His drum pupils became customers..."

necessary. His instrument was responsive to him alone; one guitarist who picked it up in the studio while still plugged in failed to get a single recognisable note out of it.

The name of Marshall has already been mentioned in conjunction with that of Eric Clapton. And just as the Les Paul would enjoy a renaissance after 'Slowhand' adopted it, so the products of amplification maker Jim Marshall would become the world-wide standard for rock guitarists.

Marshall was originally a drum teacher who opened his own musical instrument shop in London in 1960. His drum pupils became customers and brought along other members of their bands, leading to him stocking stringed instruments.

Customers for these soon apprised him of the need for an amplifier similar to the Fender Bassman, but with a gutsier sound, optimised for guitar – so, in 1962, he instigated the design of a new guitar amplifier. Engineer Ken

▲ **Gibson Les Paul Gold Top**

...Bran and designer Dudley Craven came up with a 50-watt amp that not only suited Eric Clapton down to the ground but was quickly taken up by the likes of Pete Townshend, Jimi Hendrix and Paul Kossoff. By the late 1960s, it was a very familiar sight to see a rock guitarist strutting his stuff in front of a Marshall stack.

Townshend it was who'd encouraged Marshall to develop a 100-watt amp, this necessitating a move from 2x12 to 4x12 cabs. An experimental 8x12 cab caused dissent among the Who road crew for its unwieldiness, hence the evolution of the standard 'rig' of two 4x12 cabs, the amp piggy-backed on top of the upper, slope-front cabinet. Interestingly the Marshall speaker cones stood up well to Townshend's ritual autodestruction routine: despite the impressive splintering effect, only the cloth had to be replaced at the end of the night.

The move to mighty Marshalls didn't suit everyone – Henry McCullough of Joe Cocker's Grease Band played at the legendary Woodstock festival in 1969, but didn't enjoy the experience as much as he'd hoped. "The thought of playing through a stack of Marshalls was very appealing, but it was the most uncontrollable thing I ever attempted. It just overpowered me. Back in Woodstock days it was Marshalls, Acoustics, Fender Dual Showman. In the days when Marshalls were the thing, I had a little Fender Twin sitting in the corner." Smaller amps could indeed be mixed up and put through the larger PA (public address) system with the vocals, but most guitarists preferred to be heard primarily via their backline.

(Little wonder many suffered from tinnitus or other volume-related hearing problems in later life.)

Vox and Marshall's success was noted by others, and the 1960s proved to be a golden age for the British amplifier. Orange, with their distinctively coloured cabs adopted by Fleetwood Mac, among others, and Hiwatt were just two makers' names that would become familiar to musicians and concert-goers alike. In this era, amps were invariably 'tube' or valve amplifiers: transistorisation was yet to come.

Effects, too, were to play an ever-increasing role in the guitar's sound. While players of the 1950s had nothing but a lead between their instrument and the amplifier, the 1960s saw profusion of foot-operated effects interposed in an

ROCK REARS ITS HEAD

attempt to paint new sonic landscapes. These included wah-wah (which varied the tone from trebly to bassy, giving the 'talking' effect its name suggested), echo (the previously mentioned Echoplex or Copicat), fuzz (distortion) and octave divider. Guitarist-controlled flangeing and phasing would come later.

Gibson's arrowhead-shaped Flying V had been an exotic, not to say phallic, addition to their catalogue in the late 1950s, and remained so nearly a decade later when Jimi Hendrix added it to his arsenal. He employed his hand-painted instrument most

notably in late 1967. The V had found few takers when it first appeared but heavy rockers were clearly more adventurous characters than their predecessors of nearly a decade earlier, and the later instruments (discernible by their triangle-style control layout, replacing the 'three in a row' of early examples) were fairly widely seen.

Rock players who have claimed the Flying V as a signature guitar include Andy Powell of Wishbone Ash, Dave Davies of the Kinks, Kim Simmonds of Savoy Brown, Kenny 'KK' Downing of Judas Priest and Michael Schenker, sometime

▲ **Gibson Carlos Santana SG Special**

ROCK REARS ITS HEAD

of UFO and latterly with his own Michael Schenker Group.

Another left-handed Flying V legend was Albert King – one of the three 'Kings' of blues guitar along with BB, and Freddie, all unrelated. The historical coincidence may long be debated, as may the trio's relative success and influence. But while Albert must give way to BB in terms of profile, his music, wrenched hot and steaming from his distinctively shaped Gibson V (his 'Lucy' was as dear to him as BB's 'Lucille'), was certainly influential on Eric Clapton. His 'Born Under

A Bad Sign' found its way into Cream's repertoire, while Derek and the Dominos covered 'Blues Power', to name but two songs. Johnny Winter learned licks from his early singles, while Stevie Ray Vaughan, too, was an unashamed later admirer. "I wanted to see how many places Albert's stuff would fit," he said of his work on David Bowie's 1983 monster album 'Let's Dance', "and it always does!"

On the other side of the Gibson/Fender divide, the evergreen Stratocaster had remained very recognisable despite Fender's change of management. The headstock was enlarged to counter

▲ Gibson Carlo Santana
SG Special

warping which had affected the smaller-headed instruments, while from 1967 onwards the option of a maple fingerboard was again offered. Also, the chemical formula of the nitro-cellulose finish was changed to avoid the typical 'cracking' to be found on old examples. But even this would be no proof against the abuse meted out by one James Marshall Hendrix during his brief, but bright, late 1960s heyday.

In his early days, Hendrix might buy a guitar in a local music shop before that night's gig, set it up and (ab)use it for just one night. But a white example which had been a favourite during the last two years of his life survived lighter fluid and being played by teeth to sell for £198,000 at Sotheby's in 1990. Hendrix had played the then-new instrument for the first time in

> *"In his early days, Hendrix might buy a guitar in a local music shop before that night's gig, set it up and (ab)use it for just one night."*

public at the Philharmonic Hall, New York, in November 1968, and continued to use it at festivals like Woodstock, Isle of Wight and Atlanta. After his last-ever gig in September 1970, he presented it to Experience drummer Mitch Mitchell to commemorate the birth of his daughter.

By contrast, Clapton's best-known Strat made £313,000 in 1999. So what makes Hendrix so special, apart from the fact that he bowed out at his peak? His treatment of the Strat, Flying V or whatever was typified by a desire to get music out of anything by any means. Liberal use of the whammy bar was one way, while he'd detune strings, hit the neck or manipulate controls to achieve new effects. Talking of effects, his almost voice-like wah-wah and fuzz pedal excursions influenced a whole generation of players. The Univibe, an electronic tremolo/vibrato effect, was also a favourite.

A left-hander, Hendrix invariably used right-handed instruments, turning the nut around and reversing the strings. The inconvenience of having the controls and tremolo arm at the top of the body seemed to make no difference. The three-piece instrumental format gave him the room to improvise and he used it to the full, throwing in occasional melodies like 'Strangers In The Night' while supporting his lead with an ever-changing selection of rhythm riffs on the bass strings. He pushed the envelope nearly every time he played or recorded, and it's a tribute to his success that he's spawned so many imitators.

But the biggest legacy of Jimi Hendrix was, arguably, feedback. Since the earliest days, the guitarist and recording engineer had regarded feedback –when a microphone or guitar pickup and an amplifier and speaker sets up a 'ring' of sound) as a menace. The

ROCK REARS ITS HEAD

▲ Mesa Boogie Amp

ROCK REARS ITS HEAD

Beatles daringly used it on the introduction to 'Day Tripper' because they were the Beatles and they could. Hendrix took it further; he used it, tamed it and made it a major part of his musical armoury.

While Hendrix favoured the Flying V, Eric Clapton and George Harrison both had specially painted Gibson SGs. (Clapton's, decorated by Apple's pet art group the Fool, is now owned by Todd Rundgren). He purchased the instrument, made in 1965, when two years old to replace a stolen Les Paul. He then confusingly adopted a 335 for his last days with Cream: check out 'Badge' for aural evidence.

Something else you'll hear on that track from Cream's 'Goodbye' album, coincidentally co-written by Clapton and Harrison, is the sound of the electric guitar through a Leslie speaker. More usually employed with a Hammond organ, the cabinet has a rotating arm which causes 'ripples' in the sound – a

▲ Gibson EDS-1275
(Double Neck)

relatively rarely used but nevertheless useful effect.

As Clapton overcame his addictions and rebuilt his career in low-key fashion in the early 1970s, he left his Gibsons behind and switched to Stratocasters. He fashioned his favourite, named 'Blackie', from bits of a 1957 (the body), 1956 (the neck) and early 1970s (pickups) instruments, having purchased a dozen instruments from a music shop in Nashville for $100 apiece. "At that time they were pretty unfashionable," he recalls – but with so many players taking their lead from him, it was inevitable there'd be another upsurge in popularity for a guitar whose time, many thought, had gone with Hendrix's late-1970 death.

Clapton's first guitar partner of the early 1970s had been Duane Allman, who had made his name with sibling Gregg in the Allman Brothers Band. He teamed with Clapton in Derek and the Dominos, featuring on their classic album 'Layla And Other Assorted Love Songs' (1970) to which he contributed searing slide guitar. Though a Les Paul user, Duane

"Carlos Santana's SG Special gained fame from its appearance on the Woodstock film of the 1969 festival..."

ROCK REARS ITS HEAD

preferred the Gibson SG for slide guitar thanks to its unparalleled access to the upper frets. The secret of his technique was the glass pill bottle he wore on his left-hand ring finger, resulting in a characteristic slide sound – a technique much used by blues players. Another American to coax distinctive slide riffs from the no-frills SG was Quicksilver Messenger Service's John

Cipollina. His highly customised instrument was the cover star of 'Maximum Darkness', a 1975 live album by Welsh band Man with whom he guested.

The SG, as previously mentioned, had replaced the more substantial Les Paul in production in the early 1960s and found

greatest acceptance from those who considered the Paul too heavy and

▲ Dan Armstrong Plexiglass Guitar

unmanoeuverable. Frank Zappa, for instance, was an aficionado; he typically 'hotted up' his instruments with Barcus Berry bridge pickups to obtain what he termed his "sweat hog type of sound."

Carlos Santana's SG Special gained fame from its appearance on the Woodstock film of the 1969 festival where 'Soul Sacrifice' was a showstopping highlight. He'd used it since 1965 in conjunction with a Fender Twin Reverb amp set-up for his stinging leads both live and on his band's first, eponymous album: by 'Caravanserai' he'd switched to a 1959 Les Paul,

inadvertently christening the Mesa Boogie range of amplifiers when testing out a prototype.

"Shit, man, this thing really boogies" he told inventor Randall Smith – and the rest is history.

Black Sabbath's Tony Lommi would eventually have a signature SG to his name, but back in the early 1970s when he was busy making a name for himself in Black Sabbath a stock left-hander sufficed. Lommi lost the tips of his fretting fingers while working in a manufacturing job, and was forced to wear thimbles at the ends of the affected digits: this quite possibly contributed to his heavy-riffing

ROCK REARS ITS HEAD

style that featured in such Sabbath hits as 'Paranoid'.

It may well have been Lommi's patronage that persuaded AC/DC's Angus Young to make the SG his workhorse, Certainly, the diminutive Australian, whose recording career started in 1975, would have appreciated its relatively light weight – as would band vocalists Bon Scott and (later) Brian Johnson who were obliged to carry him on their shoulders for part of the band's stage act!

The early 1970s was also the time when a Gibson SG derivative became one of the most distinctive silhouettes in rock – the double-neck guitar. The prime example of the genre is surely Jimmy Page's cherry red EDS-1275 whose 12 and six-string necks enabled him to play both the verse and solo sections of Led Zeppelin's epic 'Stairway To Heaven' on stage without having to change guitars. Page was hardly the most substantial physical specimen, but was able to tote the SG's limited bulk.

Charlie Whitney (Family) and Steve Howe (Yes) followed in Page's fingerprints with their own EDS-1275s. Their respective bands' intricate mixture of music required the versatility an instrument of this

▲ Dan Armstrong
Plexiglass Bass

kind could offer. Other British progressive-rock players to favour the double neck include Les Holroyd (Barclay James Harvest) and Mike Rutherford (Genesis). Both were bassists seeking to add more strings to their bow; Holroyd's Gibson offered a six-string alternative, while Rutherford's Shergold (a British make prevalent in the 1970s) was a four and 12-string hybrid.

John McLaughlin, Britain's foremost jazz-rock guitarist who led the Stateside-based Mahavishnu Orchestra, took delivery of his first double-neck Gibson in late 1971. Attempts to order a custom-made second guitar came to nothing, so he went to Los Angeles-based luthier Rex Bogue, whose design included pre-set volume options, a built-in pre-amp and elaborately decorated fretboards.

Rick Neilson of Cheap Trick would take the whole multi-neck fad to extremes a decade later. He had become friendly with company founder Paul Hamer during the early 1970s, when Hamer was still delivering mail in Philadelphia, and had him build him a five-neck instrument which proved a real crowd-pleaser. From top to bottom, it featured a 12-string, six string, six-string with vibrato, six-string and six-string fretless.

But that was a late 1970s/early 1980s phenomenon. In the main, the late 1960s was a time when exceptional music was being made on often unremarkable instruments.

1970s – A DECADE OF EXTREMES

If the 1960s had ended with the return of a familiar shape in the form of the Les Paul, the 1970s would be a decade of extremes. The Dan Armstrong Plexiglas guitar and bass was undoubtedly the weirdest instrument on the block. Armstrong was a New Yorker who joined forces with the Ampeg company (previously noted for its amplification) in about 1968 to produce something both ear and eye-catching – and succeeded. Interestingly, Fender had followed their see-through amplifier heads with a single example of the Duo-Sonic which was exhibited at a musical instrument trade show in 1961, but clearly (!) didn't catch on.

Though Keith Richards had a dalliance with the instrument in the mid 1970s, American rockers Tom Petty, Todd Rundgren and Randy California were among the most enthusiastic Dan Armstrong users. Petty enjoyed their visual appeal, though he'd trade his at the end of the set for a Flying V since the Gibson in question was part of his band's logo. California helped Armstrong refine the design by suggesting a metal fret be used instead of the wooden bridge, while Rundgren took maximum advantage of the guitar's transparent construction by keeping a frozen

▲ Burns Flyte

1970s – A DECADE OF EXTREMES

'ice-lolly' replica in a refrigerator backstage. For the encore, he'd take the fake guitar with him and, holding it by the 'stick' (a spare neck), would smash it on stage to the astonishment and delight of his audience.

The double cutaway Dan Armstrong only remained available for a year, having failed to attract a wide enough customer base to justify the expense of production. Plexiglas (the dense bullet-proof material helicopter windows are made out of) was far from cheap. Ampeg sensibly returned to amp manufacture.

If the Dan Armstrong had been made with looks very much in mind, then it's probably no surprise that the glam-rock boom of the early 1970s brought some strange custom-built shapes to the fore. Slade's Dave Hill was a guitarist with a Marc Bolan-inspired over-the-top image who delighted in reflecting this in his choice of guitars. Both he and his T Rex 'rival' played the futuristically-shaped Burns Flyte, a guitar whose streamlined profile was supposed to owe something to the recently introduced Concorde supersonic airliner. Sadly its performance failed to match its looks. Undaunted, Hill looked to British guitar maker John

▲ **Framus Superyob**

125

1970s – A DECADE OF EXTREMES

▲ Metal Front Tony Zematis Guitar
as Used by Marc Bolan of T-Rex

▲ Tony Zemaitis Guitar

Birch, who made him a 'Super Yob' guitar which was subsequently copied by German company, Framus. The original is now owned by Marco Pirroni of Adam and the Ants fame, as is one of the Glitter Band's 'Star Guitars'; indeed, both showed up in the video for Adam's 1984 single 'Apollo 9'.

Midlander Birch made other unique guitars for local heroes including the likes of Wizzard's Roy Wood (a shovel shape, among others) and Black Sabbath's Tony Iommi. His commission of a Gibson SG-style left-hander with 24 frets would become his most used guitar of the period.

Hill and Bolan were also clients of Tony Zemaitis, whose career as a custom guitar builder stretched from 1965 to 2000. His guitars' bodies were typically decorated with engraved gunmetal or mother of pearl-style inlays, a trademark imitated in the 1990s by Canadian company Godin with its Radiator series. Faces members Ronnie Wood and Ronnie Lane were also enthusiastic Zemaitis users, as was Groundhog Tony McPhee, but such is these unique instruments' value that very few ever now get anywhere near the concert stage due to the risk of theft.

Zemaitis may have employed metal as a decorative feature of his guitars, but American Travis Bean decided that using metal necks could be the answer to warping as well as giving greater sustain. His instruments were distinguishable by their metal 'tuning-fork' style headstocks, cut out in the middle to give the illusion of the capital letter T.

1970s – A DECADE OF EXTREMES

The neck-through-body design housed the pickups and bridge – but, though rosewood fingerboards were standard issue, few guitarists proved as adventurous as endorsee Jerry Garcia of Grateful Dead fame and, typically conservative, didn't warm to the feel of metal beneath their palms. One notable exception, interestingly, was Bill Wyman, who used a Travis Bean bass for the Rolling Stones' 'Some Girls' album and proclaimed it "probably the best bass sound I've ever had on record".

Kramer, founded by an ex-Travis Bean man associate, took up the cudgels from 1977 with a similar range of guitars and basses. Gary Kramer had joined with Travis Bean and Marc McElwee in 1974, to form Travis Bean Guitars, but quickly developed disagreements with Bean and, in October 1975 linked with musical instrument retailer Dennis Berardi to form Kramer Guitars. The resulting guitars exhibited many of the Travis Bean features, but the idea was to produce a more affordable instrument with the feel of a traditional guitar yet utilising the aluminium neck. Backers included Peter Laplaca, former vice president of Gibson parent

▲ Travis Bean Bass

company Norlin.

The first designs were the creations of Kramer, Berardi and luthier Phil Petillo, using fancy woods like burled walnut, maple and koa for the body. Bolted-on aluminium necks had a different headstock design shaped like a tuning fork, and had wood inserts to save weight. The fretboard was not wood, however, but ebonol, a patented material guaranteed not to chip, crack, warp or have any of the other problems associated with standard wood necks. Its more usual use was in the manufacture of bowling balls!

The DMZ Series aimed at the heavy metal market and introduced in 1978 were, as their name suggests, fitted with high-output twin DiMarzio humbucking pickups or three

single coils and had an offset double-cutaway body. Most revolutionary of all, however, was the Gene Simmons Axe, a signature model from 1980 whose name speaks for itself. The instrument's body was the blade and the neck the handle. As with everything Kiss-related, the guitar received much publicity (a signed, limited edition of 1,000 was produced) but its lack of appeal to non-fans gave it just a year on catalogue in both four and six-string forms.

Gary Kramer had left the company within a year, leaving Dennis Berardi and Peter Laplaca to continue under his name. Financial difficulties then beset Kramer, who would re-emerge in the following decade under the ownership of Los Angeles' Guitar Center with the likes of the Duke, a headless guitar, similar to the

1970s – A DECADE OF EXTREMES

▼ Kramer Duke

▲ Kramer DMZ Series

Steinberger, with an aluminium neck. They'd then link with rising star Eddie Van Halen, a story related in detail in chapter eight.

But not all of the decade's players were obsessed with looks. As the new wave's utilitarian ethos took hold, so the scene saw the return of some of Gibson's less heralded products that had taken their bow as far back as the 1950s. It was not so much the retro appearance of these Les Paul Juniors and Melody Makers but their combination of affordability and durability.

The Les Paul Junior, championed by Gibson chief Ted McCarty as an ideal beginner's instrument on its introduction in 1954, was an uncontoured-body mahogany guitar. The meaty tone of its single P90 pickup, light weight and playability made the Junior a favourite of Mountain's Leslie West. The tailpiece was the standard bar as used on Les Pauls since 1954, and its price-tag on introduction a modest $99. The Les Paul TV was similar but boasted a natural finish similar to that of the Telecaster, while the Special was a twin-pickup version of the TV.

By 1958, the Les Paul Juniors and Specials had become double cutaway instruments, while the all-mahogany Melody Maker, introduced in 1959, was the equivalent of Fender's Duo-Sonic, an attempt to compete further for entry-level players. Short-scale Melody Makers intended for younger players are now quite valuable. The line was eventually folded into the SG family before disappearing quietly from Gibson's

1970s – A DECADE OF EXTREMES

catalogue in the late 1960s/early 1970s.

Joan Jett, rhythm guitarist/leader of the all-girl Runaways, switched to the instrument because of its light weight (she's five feet five). "It just fits me well," she says of her 1968 Melody Maker purchased from Eric Carmen from the Raspberries. "I changed the treble pickup for a 'red velvet Hammer' pickup hand-wound by Red Rhodes and his son. I already had that pickup in my blonde Les Paul and had fallen in love with it, and so I put them in all my guitars. I love my Les Paul but it is very heavy, so that was a major reason I switched to the Melody Maker."

English manufacturer Gordon Smith took the Les Paul TV as the basis for their GS-1 and GS-2. Unlike the 'originals', their pickups could operate in both single-coil and humbucking modes, giving them sounds ranging from Fender's cutting edge to the more weighty Gibson. But these were no mere copies: the GS-1, designed to save natural resources, offered a lacquered mahogany body and mahogany neck without the irrelevant frills, and the result was a fine handmade guitar at an affordable price. Buzzcock Peter Shelley was one satisfied customer.

Gibson's 1970s products would, almost without exception, fail to make more than a minor mark. The L-6S, introduced in 1975, was unusual in extolling versatility, not usually a Gibson trait. The secret, advertisements claimed, was an exclusive 'Q system' which enabled the guitar's new 'super humbucking' pickups to be used in series, parallel and singly. Mike

▲ Gibson Melody Maker

▲ Gibson Les Paul TV

▲ Gibson RD Series

Oldfield (who was pictured with one on the cover of his 1979 album 'Exposed') and Carlos Santana were among those game enough to give it a try.

A six-position tone selector plus volume treble and mid-range controls (the only Gibson solid-body to offer the last-named) completed a Custom package advertised by Al Di Meola – probably one of the few guitarists brainy enough to appreciate "the best two guitars you'll ever play". Other, less cerebral figures simply remember the L6-S as "looking like a Les Paul that got run over", being wider and thinner than its famous relative.

The RD (research and development) series was reminiscent of a 'melted Firebird' and came in Standard, Custom and Artist configurations plus Standard and Artist basses. The latter's active electronics were impressive, including a sensitivity adjustment control which increased the instrument's "sensitivity to pick attack". Potentially more confusing was a compression/ expansion circuit, operated by a mode switch, which reduced attack and increased sustain on the rear pickup or gave a "very fast, explosive response with a rapid decay" on the bridge pickup. A unique headstock inlay combined depictions of an f-hole and a lightning bolt, the result supposedly signifying the combination of tradition and technology. Left with many unwanted RD bodies Gibson recycled some as Firebirds in the 1980s – a sad end to a potentially innovative but seemingly

1970s — A DECADE OF EXTREMES

unattractive guitar.

Having failed to attract Gibson users in the 1960s with their Coronado series of semi-acoustics, Fender had another try in 1976 with the offset-waisted Starcaster, which lasted a mere four years on catalogue. As previously mentioned, the Fenders that found the greatest favour in the 1970s were the more offbeat designs like the Jazzmaster. Elvis Costello adopted the instrument, having his name set into the fretboard in mother of pearl. At the other end of the stylistic spectrum came Television's Tom Verlaine, the nearest thing to a guitar hero the new wave could offer. His band's debut album 'Marquee Moon' saw Tom's Jazzmaster duelling most effectively with the Stratocaster of Richard Lloyd.

Meanwhile, the entry-level Fenders of the 1950s and 1960s were returning in the hands of groups like Talking Heads, whose anti rock-star stance meant they were on the lookout for anti guitar hero guitars. Thus Tina Weymouth (bass) and David Byrne (rhythm guitar) could be ironic instrumentalists. New counterparts to the Mustang and Bronco were to appear in 1979 as the Lead I and Lead

▲**Fender Starcaster**

135

II, but these proved the latest in a long line of Fender flops.

Hamer were to become a hot new name on the block as the 1970s wore on. Their initial design showed a leaning towards the Gibson school of thought, with the Standard (favoured by the previously mentioned Rick Neilsen of Cheap Trick) owing much to the Explorer. When Cheap Trick toured with the Runaways in 1976-77, he 'converted' their Lita Ford to the instrument, which received much photographic attention until the winsome Ms Ford transferred her affections to BC Rich.

Hamer's twin humbucker-loaded double-cutaway Sunburst was like a more luxurious Les Paul Junior, while a 1981 Prototype found favour with Police man Andy Summers. Former postman Paul Hamer would go on to deliver some quietly interesting guitars in the 1980s, but, after Hamer himself bowed out and the company was taken over by Ovation in the late 1980s, they joined the Superstrat pack.

Japanese manufacturers had taken advantage of slipping standards among the American 'name guitar' manufacturers to carve their own share of the

▲ Hamer Standard

1970s — A DECADE OF EXTREMES

market. Arai and Ibanez were good and, in some ways, contrasting examples. Arai were founded by Shiro Arai, a classical guitarist in the 1950s and issued guitars under the Arai, Aria and Diamond names. They are credited as starting the copy phenomenon in the late 1960s, appreciating that a quick-off-the-mark manufacturer could profit from the situation where Eric Clapton and Peter Green had stimulated a demand for the Les Paul that Gibson were unable (and, at first, seemingly unwilling) to fulfil.

The first Japanese-made Les Paul copy was followed by Telecaster-alikes and, unusually, versions of the Dan Armstrong The first major original design from Aria (the most used appellation) came in the shape of the Pro II, a three pickup item available in several options. However, the lack of impact the design made was possibly indicated by the endorsee involved – Boomtown Rat Gerry Cott. But Aria hung in there, remaining in business into the new millennium with a mixture of Strat-alikes and more exotic shapes ranging from BC Rich-alikes to near-replicas of the Gibson Explorer.

The Explorer,

▲ Aria Pro II

▼ Small Body GB-10 Signature Model for George Benson

▲ Ibanez Destroyer

1970s – A DECADE OF EXTREMES

like Gibson's Flying V and, arguably, the Les Paul, had been relatively unappreciated in its day and would be revived several times after its original (and very short) late-1950s production run. Its body shape was angular in the extreme, huge upper and lower horns making it almost star-shaped, while the combination of korina (light coloured mahogany) wood and gold hardware making it a poser's dream. The Explorer's droopy headstock was arguably the father of the 'pointy' examples prevalent in the 1980s, but the design as a whole would prove just as influential on the likes of Ibanez's Destroyer.

The first Ibanez instruments had appeared as long ago as 1932, but it took four decades to make a mark on the outside world, initially with copies of the Gibson SG and Les Paul and then similar Fender clones. The push towards original designs had already begun when, in 1977, Gibson's parent company Norlin played tough and sued Ibanez's owners for infringement of their copyright. They responded by making signature models for George Benson (the GB-10 and GB-20 arch-tops), and Steve Miller (the solid-body Artist), indicating their wish to gather credibility.

Kiss were a major band of the 1970s, combining face paint and outrageous stage antics with passable hard rocking riffs. Their major solid design of the time, the Destroyer, was tied in with Kiss's Paul Stanley, an endorsement that led to many fans like Eddie Van Halen purchasing the instrument. It didn't matter that the lines were incredibly familiar – as with Hamer's Standard, the long since discontinued Gibson Explorer being the inspiration.

The Destroyer found immediate acceptance with players in the New Wave of British Heavy Metal like Phil Collen, originally of Girl and later of Def Leppard. The guitar's angular lines contrasted effectively with the Les Pauls favoured by his Leppard partner Steve Clark. He particularly praised the tremolo which "just won't go out of tune", but added a DiMarzio Super Distortion pickup to emulate his own Les Paul and give the best of both worlds – visual impact and sonic satisfaction.

Though the Yamaha company dated from the 19th century and had begun guitar manufacture shortly after World War II, they took their time entering the electric market. Their mid to late-1960s products like the SG-5 and semi-acoustic SA-15 were typified by their unusual lines including projecting lower horns – always an eye-catching feature, if somewhat disconcerting at first.

More original solid-body options followed, but even Yamaha must have been surprised at the speed and extent of the success of their SG-2000. Introduced in 1976, it owes its breakthrough squarely to Carlos Santana, who adopted the marque as his own. He had been an aficionado of Gibson solid-bodies, having played SG, L-6S and the Les Paul, so perhaps it wasn't surprising to find the new guitar shared many of the latter's sterling qualities – though differing immediately by having an upper as well as lower cutaway (possibly the source of the SG appellation?) Santana's own instruments boasted

1970s – A DECADE OF EXTREMES

▼ Yamaha SA-15

▲ Yamaha SG-5

intricate inlays on the fretboard, while Ultravox's Midge Ure was another noted musician to play the 'stock' version.

The Yamaha SG-2000 didn't so much result from a revolution but an evolution. In taking the strong points of the existing Les Paul and throwing in twists like the through neck and double cutaway for good fret access, it showed the way to future makers like Paul Reed Smith. After all, when Gibson and Fender had got things so right, whether by accident or design, why throw the baby out with the bath water? Something built with obvious care could always rival the big names who were perceived to be in an indifferent spell.

Yamaha are best known today for their excellent Pacifica range of Strat-style guitars which range from entry-level models to 'signatures', but it has to be said that nothing has yet approached the SG-2000 in terms of professional acceptance.

Many young guns of the era looked to the past in the search for eye-catching shapes. The Gretsch White Falcon was seen in the hands of players as diverse

▲ Yamaha SG-2000

1970S – A DECADE OF EXTREMES

▲ Ovation Breadwinner

▲ Gretsch White Falcon

s Billy Duffy of the Cult, Stray Cat
Brian Setzer, Elvis Costello and
U2's the Edge. Of the newer
designs, the Ovation Breadwinner
was, as its name suggests, a victor –
f not a money-maker for its
manufacturer.

It was the result of the American
acoustic guitar manufacturer
trying to grab a share of the
lucrative electric market and not
quite getting it right. In 1988,
they'd stop trying and buy
themselves an established
performer in Hamer, but the
Breadwinner and slightly more
luxurious Deacon (of which Steve
Marriott was an endorsee)
entertained the early-1970s crowds.

They shared a futuristic look,
akin to a melting axehead, but
more significantly boasted built-in
pre-amps – the first production

American guitars to venture into
onboard 'active' electronics. (Aria
caught the vibe with their retro-
styled M-650T in the late 1990s.)
The single cutaway Viper and
double Preacher were less
extraordinary-looking, but
similarly failed to catch on. A
venture into Superstrats in the
1980s proved equally unsuccessful,
though Ovation electrics are now
highly prized for their build
quality.

Amplifiers of the period had
advanced apace from the days of
Vox and Marshall; now graphic
equalisation was standard on pro-
standard amps, allowing he sound
to be tailored to individual taste.

The introduction of
transistorised amplifiers in the late
1960s and 1970s was hailed as both
a revolution and a boon for

▲ Mesa Boogie Amp

1970s — A DECADE OF EXTREMES

guitarists. There was, for instance, a substantial weight saving. Master volume amplifiers were promoted as an answer to creating valve-like distortion, but a later solution was 'tube pre-amps', available in stomp-box form.

Bass players have by and large adopted solid-state (transistorised) amplification as standard. But in the same way as the virtues of the Les Paul were realised only after its discontinuation, so valve amplifiers were only truly appreciated by six-string players after they had been superseded and manufacture had slowed or ceased. Early transistor amps were often unreliable or had a sound that compared unfavourably with the warmth of the old-fashioned 'bottles'.

The hottest name in guitar amplification in the 1970s was the Mesa Boogie, developed by San Francisco's Randy Smith, who used souped-up circuits and different combinations of valves in a three-stage system to become the professional guitarist's amp of choice.

In parallel with developments in the field of amplification, there grew a trade in high output replacement pickups designed to 'hot-rod existing guitars.

▲ **Aria M-650T**

▼ Ovation Preacher

▲ Ovation Viper

Now-familiar names like DiMarzio and Seymour Duncan appeared on the market at this time, their products designed to slot into the spaces their factory-fitted predecessors had occupied (most guitarists are, sensibly, still wary of modifying their instruments in a non-reversible way).

One of the effects that will always be associated with the 1970s is the talkbox, a favourite of Peter Frampton and sometime Eagle Joe Walsh. Frampton's live album 'Comes Alive' (1976) contained many crowd-pleasing solos featuring the effect, which channelled the sound into the guitarist's mouth to be exhaled into the vocal microphone. He now markets his own Framtone talkbox which he uses on the live performance of songs like 'Show Me The Way'. Walsh's best-known composition featuring the effect was 'Rocky Mountain Way'.

Having spent six chapters following the evolution of the six-string guitar, in true Biblical fashion we'll take a rest from our task and catch up with what had been going on inthe four-string world.

"One of the effects that will always be associated with the 1970s is the talkbox, a favourite of Peter Frampton and sometime Eagle Joe Walsh."

BASS-IC MATTERS

Having given electric guitar players the license to play at loud volume, Leo Fender now had to even up the argument. The standard 'doghouse' bass would not be able to compete, so the logical next move was to adapt the Telecaster to give bassists a shot. His desire, he would tell writer Tom Wheeler, was "to free the bass player from the big acoustic bass. The thing was usually confined to the back of the band, and the bass player couldn't get up to the mike to sing."

As ever, the man got it spot-on. Fully half a decade on from his first effort, the instrument he came up with is still around in almost exactly the same form as originally devised. There are other shapes, plus five and even six-string instruments available, while the outlandish Chapman Stick is like no other stringed instrument in appearance and ability – but for most players it's the Fender bass that still rules supreme. Even given bassists' innate conservatism, that's quite some accolade.

The first Precision (as Fender named it) appeared in 1951 with a price tag just 50 cents short of a round $200. To all intents and purposes, it looked like a scaled-up Tele with a 34-inch neck and, with an ash body and simple maple neck, was similar in construction. The

▲ Gibson EB-1 Bass

BASS-IC MATTERS

trings were tuned in familiar E-A-D-G fashion like the double bass, and were amplified via a simple four-pole pickup governed by volume and tone control knobs.

The instrument's down-to-earth name came from the fact that, with frets at his disposal, the bassist could now guarantee to hit the note accurately every time as opposed to sliding into it as on a stand-up instrument. In Leo Fender's words, the concept was "simple. If a player noted the right fret, the tone was right-on: a precision result." (This also gave guitarists who wanted to double on the instrument

less of a transition problem.)

Yet the move from acoustic stand-up bass to a new-fangled, unconventional instrument would prove far from easy for the relatively conservative bass-playing fraternity. Monk Montgomery, brother of guitarist Wes, was probably typical of the breed. Then employed as a backing musician to vibes-player Lionel Hampton, he told Guitar Player magazine that, when 'Hamp' first handed him the brand-new Fender, telling him he wanted to use an electric bass in the band line-up, "It was like he was trying to turn me on to another chick!" The Fender,

▲ Gibson EB-2 Bass

151

he explained, was considered "a bastard instrument…conventional bass players despised it. It was new, and a threat to what they knew."

Eventually, though, and despite his affection for his upright, Monk succumbed. "I had no choice – I wanted the job," he reasoned. "I felt bad, but it was a challenge. Before and after each gig I would sit in my room and play the electric. It's tuned the same way as the upright but physically it was different. Strings, size, the way that you hold it, the tension. I had to get used to it…but I made up

my mind to do it, and I did it well.".

Fender gave the electric bass commercial acceptance, that is certain. But historians aver that he was neither first to amplify the instrument, nor the first to offer a fretted alternative to the 'doghouse'. Lloyd Loar came up with an amplified 'stick' instrument in the 1920s, while the following decade saw Paul Tutmarc offer a fretted 'Audiovox' bass played like a guitar. Maybe the time just wasn't right for these two inventions, and it's certain the men behind them didn't have the success of the Telecaster to 'piggy-back' their innovation to

▲ Epiphone Rivoli Bass

success.

It's not widely realised the Fender's deadly rivals, Gibson, produced a fretted bass for some 20 years in the 1910s and 1920s. The pear-shaped Mando-Bass had a similar string length to a double bass but, though played like a guitar with a rod projecting from the underside to provide support, the sound just did not project enough to make it a viable ensemble instrument

Perhaps it was the advent of war that stopped Gibson and Rickenbacker from making more of their own adventures into the lower end of music. Gibson had followed up the Mando-Bass with two hollow-body 'Electric Bass Guitars' in 1938 which, at five feet in height, were clearly designed to be played vertically. Rickenbacker's

Electro Bass-Viol was metal-bodied and perched on top of its own amplifier, the connection being cleverly (if a little precariously) made via the pin on its base slotting into a socket.

In any event, the ability for a guitarist to adapt quickly and easily to the instrument would prove a key component of the Fender bass's success. With large jazz ensembles downsizing due to post-war austerity, guitar players needed to be adaptable – and the precise intonation offered was an obvious bonus. The scale length was a mere 34 inches compared with 40-42 inches on the 'doghouse' but was, of course, rather longer than the Telecaster's 25.5 inch fretboard.

As you would expect, Gibson responded to the advent of the

BASS-IC MATTERS

Precision by launching a range of their own basses. They were hamstrung, however, by the selection of a 30-inch scale: this would prove a boon to bassists with small hands, but did not prove attractive for the majority of players who wanted the depth a long-scale instrument offered.

The first Gibson bass to appear in 1953, two years post-Precision, was the small, violin-bodied EB-1, an instrument (advertised under the slogan 'A Revelation in Rhythm') which hedged its bets by including an extending pin for upright playing if required. It even had a fake f-hole painted on to its solid body! This lack of faith in the electric bass as a stand-alone instrument was also reflected in the numbers produced – less than 100 per year before production ceased in 1958. (It would enjoy a brief revival in the early 1970s.) Not an impressive start…

The EB-1 was followed on to the Kalamazoo production line in 1958 by the EB-2, resembling the semi-acoustic ES-335 in its shape (British beatsters like the Animals' Chas Chandler and the Searchers' Frank Allen went for its cheaper Epiphone version, the Rivoli), while 1959

▲ Gibson EB-0

brought the EB-0 development of the solid-bodied Les Paul Junior six-string guitar.

Neither newcomer offered anything distinctive enough to establish it as a front-line instrument though, when the EB-0 was restyled in 1960 to reflect the newly introduced SG, the resulting EB-3 would attract the like of Jack Bruce. Even if its two pickups offered a boomy, indistinct sound when compared to Fender's market leader, the instrument clearly offered the gifted Scot possibilities in the spacious instrumental trio format of Cream.

Bruce had

stumbled on his second-hand EB-3 in a London music shop and was attracted by its wide neck. He'd previously favoured the Fender Bass VI, a six-stringed bass with correspondingly narrow spacing between strings, and an upright he occasionally used in the studio, as on 'Fresh Cream's 'Four Until Late'. He claimed his reason for abandoning the Bass VI was that Dutch artists the Fool had given it a psychedelic paint job similar to that on bandmate Eric Clapton's Gibson SG, "but it was done the night before we left on tour…and never dried!"

In 1957, the Fender Precision received its first – and, so far, only –

▲ Gibson EB-3

makeover. The body shape was curved and contoured to more closely resemble the Stratocaster guitar. The headstock, too, became a larger facsimile of the Strat rather than the Tele's distinctively flattened profile. The 'straight across' pickup gave way to a distinctive split item, though many owners have reinstated this as a second, additional pickup nearer the bridge to add both 'oomph' and tonal variation.

The original 'slabby' body style would return to the catalogue in the late 1960s as the Telecaster Bass (in effect, a new name for the original Precision) when new owners CBS looked to extract every money-earning idea they could from their glorious past catalogue. The Telecaster Bass achieved some notoriety in the 1990s due to its use by Sting,

whose signature model (with single-coil pickup, unlike the reissue series which went humbucker in 1972) is currently a best-seller.

Worth a mention in passing is the clearly Precision-inspired Burns Bison, manufactured in Britain between 1962 and 1965 with three pickups and a range of sound options including one labelled 'Wild Dog'! Used by the likes of the Shadows, its exaggerated body horns and scalloped headstock have given it a retro-value exploited by relaunches in the 1980s and 1990s.

A big breakthrough in bass sound came in 1963 with the development of the roundwound string by James How. The new variety differed from the hitherto ubiquitous flatwound in that the

BASS-IC MATTERS

▲ Fender Bass VI

BASS-IC MATTERS

wire wrapped round the 'core' was circular in cross-section rather than flat, resulting in a much brighter tone. The only people retaining flatwounds tended to be those who wanted to emulate the upright's distinctive 'thud' and fretless players for whom the new string proved too abrasive to their fretboards.

Fender's bass was accompanied by a new amplifier that paralleled its quantum leap. The Bassman combined 26 watts of 'tube' power with a 15-inch speaker – three inches wider than the biggest available in a guitar amp at that time – through which to pump out the volume.

The Fender Precision became so ubiquitous that the Musicians Union adopted the term as generic, referring to all electric basses as

Fender bass. However, the wide neck and lack of adaptability in the single pick-up configuration led to the introduction in 1959 of a more sophisticated instrument, known as the Jazz Bass. As it happened, this would prove something of a misnomer, as it received no greater acceptance in the jazz world than any other area of music. It would, however, become widely seen over the next decade, though never rivalling its predecessor in popularity.

The Jazz would prove even more attractive to guitar players, its neck being significantly narrower at the nut (headstock end). Though a measurement of 1 7/16 inch may seem a little less than the Precision's 1 3/4 inch neck, the feel was radically different. There were crucial differences at the body end, too: a pair of pickups replaced the

BASS-IC MATTERS

▲ Fender Telecaster Bass

▼ Fender Telecaster Bass
"Sting" Signature Model

BASS-IC MATTERS

Precision's single unit, these resembling the original in their straight-across styling. The body itself was offset to resemble the newly introduced Jazzmaster six-string – hence, perhaps, the choice of name.

Early Jazz Basses had two 'stacked pots', each controlling the volume and tone of their respective pick-up. By 1962, however, a three-knob design had been adopted which adopted a separate and all-governing tone control – a sophisticated way of saying a potentiometer which cut the treble response of each pickup. Mixing the two, however, offered a surprising range of sounds when compared with the alternative.

The Fender bass, in Precision and Jazz varieties, has written its signature sound over most of the greatest music to be made from the 1960s onwards. Much of that, of course, was coming out of the United States – and when it came to the continent where rock was born, Fender had it covered from coast to coast.

In Detroit, Michigan, Motown bass ace James Jamerson had been quick to utilise the power of the Precision to move the feet. His bass lines featured on so many soul classics from 1962 onwards it's impossible to

▲ Fender Jazz Bass

count them. Motown's writing and production teams realised they had a priceless ally in creating 'The Sound Of Young America' and, rather than subjugating his flair, encouraged him to express it.

A DVD released in 2003, The Funk Brothers, paid tribute to the Motown backroom team, of which he was a part, and their contribution to countless legendary releases. Sadly such recognition came too late for Jamerson, who died in 1983 with a sense of injustice that he had been insufficiently rewarded. (interestingly, Paul McCartney would credit Jamerson as a major bass-playing influence because of his melodic sense; the other was Beach Boy Brian Wilson "because he went to unusual places.")

On the West Coast, Carol Kaye was the queen of the bass line, again preferring the Precision. Everyone from the Beach Boys to Frank Sinatra via Simon and Garfunkel knew and used her telephone number, and her legendary status endures. Joe Osborn was among others to follow in her footsteps.

Not everyone could afford a 'name' bass, of course, and as with the six-string scene there were many makers happy to help out the impecunious would-be player. America's biggest producer of guitars. Harmony came up with the single-cutaway H22, familiar to fans of the Spencer Davis Group whose Muff Winwood was a user. Danelectro also weighed in with the Longhorn and Shorthorn bass, popular in the early 1960s, and the UB2 six-string, a hybrid instrument tuned an octave below a standard guitar which Duane Eddy favoured. Longhorn users included Episode Six's Roger Glover, later of Deep Purple, while the video age saw many emerge from their cases once again thanks to the instrument's undoubted visual appeal.

Fender's line of student instruments, introduced from 1956 in an attempt to catch the beginners' market, branched out into basses in the mid 1960s when the recently introduced Mustang guitar was joined by a four-string equivalent. These short-scale items were considered inferior to the Precision, and rightly so – but a number of players with smaller fingers would make use of the instruments, particularly the Mustang, through the years to such a stage that the design was re-introduced to production in the 21st century.

Bill Wyman of the Rolling Stones was nagged by Keith Richards to play a Fender. "But they're simply too big for me. I tried a couple of Jazz Basses, but I ended up giving 'em away. So when I heard about the short-scale Mustang, I thought I'd finally be able to manage a Fender – and please Keith at the same time! It wasn't too bad. I used it on stage a bit, but it never felt quite right." Bill can be seen with a Lake Placid blue, painted-headstock Mustang in the Stones' 1970 concert film, Gimme Shelter. Status Quo's Alan Lancaster and Tina Weymouth of Talking Heads/Tom Tom Club fame were among the Mustang's other adherents, while an even more basic instrument – the entry-level Musicmaster Bass, marketed with a matching amplifier –

appeared in 1970.

Bill Wyman had started his professional life playing a Japanese bass which he rendered fretless after acquiring it while playing in R&B band the Cliftons in 1961. "Before that I'd been playing bass on the bottom two strings of a detuned guitar, so I was glad to finally have a 'real' bass. Unfortunately, it was bloody horrible!" The body was too large – but, having seen Gibson and Fender basses in pictures of Little Richard's and Fats Domino's bands, he drew an approximate shape on the back of his bass and his next-door neighbour cut it down.

"Then I bevelled the edges, took off all the paint and put in a new Baldwin pickup. Still, it rattled with every note because the frets were so worn. I figured I'd just pull out all the frets and put in new ones when I could afford some. But it suddenly sounded really good, so I never put frets back in." The instrument, possibly the first fretless electric ever, was used on every Stones album and many singles up to 1975. "Even without an amp, it sounds wonderful—it's got the sound."

Next stop was a semi-acoustic Framus Star Bass in 1964, due to its suitability for his small hands. "It was the only one

▲ **Danelectro UB2 Six String Bass**

BASS-IC MATTERS

in the shops with necks as narrow as my fretless," Wyman explains, "and the boys liked the sound on-stage; it cut through but was still boomy." He then moved on to a smaller Framus, shaped like a Les Paul with an attractive striped wood grain finish.

It's ironic that Paul McCartney, the most influential rock and pop bass player outside of the United States, never used a Fender. It's certain that his style shaped generations that followed, yet his first serious bass (and the one with which he remains connected to this day) was a relatively cheap German instrument.

The small-bodied, semi-acoustic Hofner Violin Bass was his choice initially because, being left-handed, he could turn a right-handed version over and play it without looking "stupid".

It was also a 'copy guitar', being a European (and therefore cheaper) version of Gibson's EB-0. He bought his first one in Hamburg during the Beatles' second Star Club sojourn there in 1961. "Fenders were around £100, even then, and all I could, afford was about £30," confesses the current multi-millionaire. He would continue using the instrument until the Beatles retired from touring in 1966, commending its

▲ Fender Mustang Bass

lightness which allowed him to move around the stage relatively unhindered.

McCartney moved on to the Rickenbacker 4001 in 1967, the year the Beatles produced their myth-making studio creation 'Sgt Pepper's Lonely Hearts Club band'. He could now, of course, afford left-handed instruments which, by that time, were readily available even to UK players. His Ricky, originally orange in finish, acquired a custom psychedelic paint job during the Summer of Love but survived into the 1970s, having been stripped back to the natural wood.

The 4001, a through-neck instrument with twin pickups (the bridge one a traditional Rickenbacker 'horseshoe' that surrounded the strings), was distinctive both visually – triangular fingerboard markers, white plastic pickguard – and sonically. Its predecessor the single pickup 4000 (introduced 1957) lacked its successor's bound body and fingerboard, and also had simple dot fret markers. The 4001S, the model McCartney bought, also had this rather more austere specification.

With McCartney leading the way, bass players were now appreciating they could make musical things happen instead of having to tag along underneath and play

▲ Hofner Violin Bass

the root notes of each and every chord. No longer would the bass player necessarily be the least able guitarist, but could cut loose and play counter-melodies. This freedom paved the way for the progressive rock of the following decade.

Probably the most influential player of a Rickenbacker bass after McCartney was Yes's Chris Squire. His determination to be a lead bass player like John Entwistle made use of the Ricky's trebly tone, and he was imitated by the likes of Geddy Lee (Rush). Lee's armoury of instruments included two Rickenbacker double-necks, a six-string/bass and a 12-string/bass.

Guild was a popular name in the States whose reputation rested largely on acoustic guitars. Their Starfire bass, however, was a favourite with influential US rock players Chris Hillman (Byrds, Flying Burrito Brothers) and Jack Casady (Jefferson Airplane). Ken Whaley of British group Help Yourself bought one from Jethro Tull bass player Glenn Cornick and was entranced. "It had the most perfect neck, very slim almost like a violin – and, unlike the similar Gibson and Epiphone semis of the time, it wasn't flabby or boomy but had a very wide tone range with plenty of bite. My dream guitar…"

Guild's asymmetric S-70D guitar spawned the less well known B-301/2 bass, produced in both fretless and fretted versions and with one and two pickups respectively. Guild later lent its name to the Ashbory Bass, a tiny (18-inch scale) bass with a small body, under-bridge-mounted pickup and rubber strings which was the brainchild of British designers Nigel Thornbory and Alun Jones. Seen as a gimmick by some but in reality capable of accurately imitating a double bass, it remained in production from 1987-89, but was later reclaimed by Ashbory and manufactured in a revised form with a bigger body.

Gibson had tried one last time to infiltrate the bass market with a four-stringed version of a successful guitar. Their Thunderbird bass borrowed the contours of the Firebird and, finally, had dropped the short-scale neck to go head to head with the Precision. Ken

Whaley, who bought one from Badfinger's Tommy Evans, praised its sound: "very full and resonant, like a piano's bass strings." Its through-neck design was even ahead of its time, though this was dropped for a glued neck in the mid 1960s at the same time as the guitar's advertised "ultra-modern shape" was changed to the 'non-reverse'. (Mott the Hoople's Overend Watts was a proponent, while many latter-day 'hair' bands have introduced it to the metal scene.)

Meanwhile, Jack Bruce's adventures on the EB-3 had led to some belated

▲ Framus Star Bass

BASS-IC MATTERS

▲ Rickenbacker 4001 Bass

▼ Rickenbacker 4001s Bass

popularity for Gibson basses in heavy metal circles. Mountain's Felix Pappalardi, who produced Cream's 1967 breakthrough 'Disraeli Gears', adopted an EB-1 violin bass and was its highest-profile user in the early 1970s when, coincidentally or not, it returned to production. Free's Andy Fraser was another who swam against the tide by favouring short-scale Gibsons, the muffled, boomy sound proving effective in what, like Cream and Mountain, was a guitar-bass-drums line-up (albeit with a dedicated vocalist). His imaginative basslines provided the foundation for such classics as 'All Right Now', 'Mr Big' and 'The Stealer'.

As rock pushed the envelope in the late 1960s and early 1970s, so the bass player became less of an anchor man and more of an innovator. The leader in this charge was the late John Entwistle of the Who. Even in the band's 1960s releases his bass was fighting Pete Townshend's guitar for mastery in the three-minute pop single context. His most famous 'lead break' came on 1965's 'My Generation', where the middle eight was dominated by his swooping runs and typified the trebly tone and fluid, multi-note style he favoured.

Entwistle used all ten fingers in his playing, largely due to a classical training which encompassed not only piano but trumpet (which developed his right hand fingering) and French horn (the left). He was also unwilling to yield the spotlight he'd enjoyed when playing in youth orchestras – he won a place at the Royal Academy of Music,

BASS-IC MATTERS

but couldn't afford to go – yet, with typical bloody-mindedness, decided to change the bass's function rather than switch to an acknowledged lead instrument.

Entwistle helped redefine the role of the bass guitar in rock– to the extent that, when an unknown Noel Redding was asked in 1966 to switch from six strings to four to back Jimi Hendrix, he called to ask what gear John used. "Rotosounds, Marshall amps and a Jazz Bass," came the affable reply – but his technique couldn't be bought off the shelf.

For some reason, the Jazz Bass proved the instrument of choice for reggae's top bassline exponents. Both Aston 'Family Man' Barrett and Robbie Shakespeare favoured the instrument, which means that the Jazz must feature on at least 80 per cent of Jamaica's Top 100 recordings. Barrett made up the Wailers' rhythm section with drummer brother Carlton, their close relationship legendary, while Shakespeare and drummer Sly Dunbar played the sessions they didn't.

Black music had moved on from Motown, which had passed its peak by the late 1960s, and was looking for fresh fields to conquer. In the

▲ Guild S-70D

vanguard of change was Sly and the Family Stone whose bassist, Larry Graham, was one of the first players to develop a percussive slapping and popping sound. Using just a stock mid-1960s Jazz Bass, Graham developed a technique he'd created while a club musician when his group's drummer left and he was saddled with being the entire rhythm section.

Graham's torch would be taken up by the likes of Louis Johnson and Verdine White, respectively of the Brothers Johnson and Earth Wind and Fire. Indeed, Johnson would be one of Quincy Jones' studio hands as he helped Michael Jackson make his mark on music and culture.

In a curious echo of Graham, Mark King, who led UK jazz-funk hitmakers Level 42, started his musical life as a drummer and adopted a highly percussive style. King worked with British luthier John Diggins to create the JayDee Supernatural series with through-neck construction, active electronics and an ebony fretboard which, combined with Trace Elliot amplification and King's thumb, created a formidable sound– a serious competitor to the all-conquering Alembic basses.

One of King's 1980s chart contemporaries was Peter Hook of New Order. He used his band's synthesiser-based sound as a backdrop to play what effectively was 'lead bass', often using a relatively inexpensive, British-made Shergold Marathon in trademark low-slung style (Genesis's Mike Rutherford was the other most famous user, though

BASS-IC MATTERS

his instrument of choice was a less wieldy 12-string doubleneck.)

Leo Fender may have bowed out of the company that bears his name as CBS rushed in, but he was far from finished with the musical instrument business. And it was at the bass end of things that he was to make by far his biggest post-CBS mark with the Music Man StingRay.

When he sold out in 1965, Fender was obliged to agree to a decade in which he was forbidden to compete with the company that bore his name. When this clause ran out, he predictably re-emerged as the head honcho at Music Man guitars, a company set up three years earlier by ex-employee Tom Walker and Forrest White. The most famous guitar they produced was associated with Eddie Van

Halen, and is discussed elsewhere, but their first production model, the StingRay, was considerably more successful in its four-stringed variant.

While reflecting Fender's favoured styling with double cutaway and a longer upper horn, the StingRay bass was very much its own instrument. The most obvious recognition feature was the trademarked headstock configuration, with three tuning keys at the top and one at the bottom (six-stringers split four and two). More crucially than cosmetically, the StingRay was the first production bass to feature active electronics in a treble and bass boost facility (active mid was an option), a large humbucking pickup being set within a graceful asymmetric pickguard. The result was a classic, available with an

BASS-IC MATTERS

▲ **Gibson Thunderbird Bass**

alder, ash or poplar body. Many detail improvements have since been made, including a six-bolt neck attachment, contoured body, superior neck truss-rod system, improved bridge and quieter electronics.

The StingRay proved popular with disco and funk artists, Bernard Edwards powering both Chic and a host of clients ranging from Diana Ross to Sister Sledge with a stock example. But the likes of King Crimson's Tony Levin were equally happy to endorse the instrument as a progressive rock tool: it seemed the Precision had finally been rivalled as the definitive electric bass, and ironically by a product of the man who'd started it all. (A double pickup version, the Sabre, never really took off.)

String manufacturer Ernie Ball took over Music Man in the mid 1980s and operations were moved to a new plant in the coastal town of San Luis Obispo, California, in 1985. The StingRay 5 was the first all-new Music Man bass to be designed and built there, and emerged in 1987. The 5-string's styling was based on the Silhouette guitar, with dual humbuckers that could be split to produce 10 tone combinations. A three-band graphic equaliser completed

▲ JayDee Supernatural

the package.

Leo Fender left Music Man in 1980 to form G&L Guitars with George Fullerton and Dale Hyatt. The L-2000 bass was his own take on an advanced MusicMan, with two large humbuckers, complex active electronics and also – strange as it may seem – a Kahler vibrato unit. It was a long way from the Precision, 30 years old and still the world's best-selling bass, but Leo justified his 'tinkering' with the maxim: "I owe it to musicians to make better instruments."

The fretted Precision Bass – Leo's great gift to the four-string world – had made great play of its perfect intonation, but it wasn't to the taste of every player. Jaco Pastorius was the man who single (or should that be double?)

handedly put a fretless Fender on the Christmas list of thousands of players worldwide in the mid 1970s. His dad had been a drummer, which may account for his percussive tendencies and, until picking up the bass age 15, he'd intended following in his father's footsteps.

Jaco's manipulation of a fretless Jazz Bass first came to public attention in 1976 when he joined jazz-rock fusionists Weather Report. Coincidentally or not, his six-year spell in the ranks saw the band enjoy its greatest commercial success, the single 'Birdland' all but becoming an unlikely chart item. His impact was such that Toto founder-member David Hungate, now a Nashville session ace, divides electric bass playing into 'Before Jaco' and 'After Jaco' periods. "No other individual has so totally revolutionised and expanded the approach to an instrument."

Joni Mitchell allowed him another context in which to display his brilliance, while, Pastorius's eponymous solo album – released in 1976, the quarter-century of the Fender Bass – became a touchstone for a generation. Yet his life was to end prematurely and senselessly in 1987 after a bar-room brawl. Perhaps his only subsequent counterpart was Welshman Pino Palladino, who has wielded his fretless in the service of everyone from Paul Young (whose 1980s hits prominently features his Music man StingRay) to the Who. His recruitment to the service of Daltrey and Townshend in 2002 came in the most tragic of circumstances, however, after John Entwistle's pre-tour death.

The first production fretless bass had been made not by Fender but Ampeg, whose AUB-1 arrived on the scene in 1965-66. Its semi-solid construction with pseudo-classical scrolled headstock, f-holes in both front and back and a lack of visible pickup (a transducer was mounted under the bridge) made it a less than macho proposition for the average rock bassist. The two very definitely not average players most often pictured with the instrument were Rick Danko of the Band (who modified his with Fender pickups) and Boz Burrell of Bad Company, the latter possibly employing it as an antidote to the hard-rock situation the former jazzer found himself in. Certainly, his swooping lines made hard-rock songs like 'Feel Like Makin' Love' that little bit out of the ordinary,

Ampeg (who also manufactured

BASS-IC MATTERS

▲ Musicman Stingray

BASS-IC MATTERS

a small number of four-strings modelled on the Plexiglas Dan Armstrong guitar, briefly favoured by Jack Bruce) were better known for their bass amplification systems. Most notable was the SVT which, with its 300-watt output through two 8x10 cabinets, was ideal for stadium gigs played by the likes of the Grateful Dead and Rolling Stones, who were endorsees.

With the advent of the superstar bassist came instruments fit for such creatures. Alembic was quick to see the gap in the market and, having originally been established in the 1960s as a custom shop servicing the Grateful Dead's

guitar-related needs, were a known name. The catalyst for manufacturing new instruments seems to have been the arrival of luthier Rick Turner – and the instruments in which Alembic specialised were basses.

A typical Alembic bass would be manufactured from some unusual wood and boast heavy-duty brass bridge and fittings. More unusual were the LEDs or light-emitting diodes which literally lit up the fretboard – more of a crowd-pleasing device than an aid to playing. The highest-profile Alembic user was Stanley Clarke, the bass-player with Chick Corea's jazz-rock supergroup

▲ Wal Custom Bass

Return To Forever. The first time he played his Alembic, he recalled, "a new bassist was born – I could suddenly play anything I heard in my head." Mainly a stand-up player, Clarke had graduated from the semi-acoustic Gibson EB-2, which by comparison "simply wasn't allowing me to play".

Rick Turner would, in 1977, make the first graphite neck for a bass guitar, subsequently setting up the Modulus Graphite company with Geoff Gould (a San Franciscan bassist and aerospace designer) to explore the possibilities of the material. The advantages of graphite, a carbon composite used on NASA space probes, included the elimination of dead spots on the neck where the strings failed to give an even response, while clarity and sustain were also improved. Meanwhile,

Alembic continued supplying high-spec, high-price basses to those with the talent and the pockets to use them.

Britain's major contribution to the four-stringed world came in the shape of the Wal bass, the joint product of electronics guru Ian Waller and luthier Pete Stevens who joined forces in 1974 "to build the best bass guitar in the world." After building custom instruments for players like Chris Squire (Yes) and John Perry (Caravan), the duo assembled a design team to design a top-quality instrument that was adaptable for any bass player. Input from the likes of Percy Jones, John Entwistle, Pete Zorn and Rupert Hine resulted in the Wal Pro.

By the early 1980s, the Wal Custom was the staple production model, being joined by the Wal 5-

string in 1985. With the 5th string a low B and 24 frets, the bass had an incredible range. Sadly, Ian Waller died of a heart attack in 1988, but Pete Stevens pledged to continue their dream and, in 1995, introduced the first Wal 6-string bass guitar.

Users of the Wal are so dedicated they've even formed a club, the punningly named Wal-nuts United. And though Wal don't deal in endorsements as a matter of principle, famous players to have splashed out their own cash on one include Geddy Lee of Rush, Paul McCartney, Jeff Ament of Pearl Jam, Flea of the Red Hot Chili Peppers, Mick Karn (ex-Japan) and Justin Chancellor of Tool.

Like Britain, Germany made a surprise appearance at the cutting edge of bass-making in the shape of the Warwick company and their Streamer and Thumb designs. Available in four, five and six-string variations, these were impressive looking modern instruments favoured by the likes of Jack Bruce, Dave Bronze (Eric Clapton Band), John Taylor (Duran Duran) and others.

Warwick, launched in 1982 by Hans Peter Wilfer, the son of the man who'd founded guitar-maker Framus back in 1946, started with a clean slate and were able to combine investment in up-to-date machinery with the spirit of hand craftsmanship. Particularly important was the purchase of wood in complete logs or planks rather than pre-cut which ensured complete control over the look and sound of the instrument. The wood selected was stored for three to five years before use, while the

BASS-IC MATTERS

use of hardwoods (principally wenge) led to the development of a very slim neck without loss of strength. At the end of this, Warwick's angled machine heads gave not only a distinctive look but were claimed to fall at a more natural angle for the player's hand.

Even the tailpiece and bridge designs were innovative. The former combined a rapid string-change facility with the optimum break angle of the strings over the bridge which was claimed to transmit more vibration to the wood for a fuller tone and longer sustain. The bridge itself could be locked after adjustment of action, intonation and string spacing, of each string. At the other end, an adjustable nut – each string groove the head of a recessed screw – could be individually raised or lowered

A two-way truss rod allowed correction of both concave and convex neck curvature relative to the strings, removing the inconvenience of an access screw in the centre of the neck, while even the frets were made from a bronze alloy similar to that used for church bells, chosen to transmit more of the sound into the neck and thus into the pickups. These featured twin coils around a single bar magnet, combining the hum-cancelling advantages of a humbucker with the clear tone of a single

BASS-IC MATTERS

coil.

First with everything as they tended to be in the bass world, Fender had introduced a five-string instrument, the Bass V, as long ago as 1965. But being ahead of your time doesn't always prove profitable, and the instrument (whose extra string was the C above high G) was quickly discontinued. The musical development that gave the five-string a new lease of life was 1970s disco, where the synthesiser had superseded the stringed instrument on many of the hits of the era. The need was to reproduce the synth's depths on stage, so basses with an extra lower (not higher) string were soon seen. Japan's Yamaha company were responsible for the BB5000, one of the first production five-strings, which hit the market in 1984 when Nathan East (Phil Collins/Eric Clapton) was an enthusiastic endorsee.

Yamaha's through-neck BB3000S Attitude offered an alternative to a fifth string by being equipped with a Hip Shot Bass Extender, a lever that allowed the player to detune his lowest string to a C, two full tones lower than usual, in an instant. The instrument was endorsed by Billy Sheehan of soft metal stars Mr Big (and, more notably, four-

▲ Roland G-77

stringer with a post-Van Halen David Lee Roth) Sheehan's regular appearance at the top of players' popularity polls ensured a ready market for this Precision-styled instrument.

The disco and soul of the 1970s and 1980s, with its emphasis on the bottom end of the music, had brought a number of unlikely superstar bassists to the fore. Anthony Jackson, best known for his contribution to the O'Jays' 'For The Love Of Money' (which won him a writing credit) developed a number of six-string basses in conjunction with the Jackson company.

With the bass having remained at four strings for so long, the advent of five and six-string versions was far from the end of the story. Having built any number of unusual guitars for Cheap Trick's Rick Neilsen, Hamer were receptive to bandmate Tom Petersson's 1977 idea for a 12-string bass but, initially worried about the amount of tension on the neck, they started with a 10-string layout – three Gs, 3Ds (one fundamental with two octave strings) two As and two Es (one fundamental with one octave string).

Once built, Hamer felt it would prove the design concept to be unfeasible and they would then remove the two extra octave strings and build Tom an 8-string bass. But when the 10-string worked just fine, they realised Tom was right, and the Hamer Quad Bass was the world's first 12-string bass guitar. Rockpile's Nick Lowe was a user of the eight-string version, toting a cherry red example when with

BASS-IC MATTERS

Rockpile in the late 1970s; a selection of his other interesting basses can be found pictured on the cover of Nick's debut solo album, 'Jesus Of Cool'.

Another innovation came from Roland, whose G77 MIDI bass system appeared in 1985. But it proved particularly difficult to translate the low-frequency vibrations of the strings into something usable by the MIDI synthesiser and was even less widely used than its six-string counterpart. (Dave Bronze, playing with electronic band the Art of Noise in 1986, cleverly transposed his samples down an octave which enabled him to play more accurately one octave above!) Another answer to the problem, the Peavey Midibase (sic) of 1992, employed sensors in the fingerboard and a rack-mounted interface that could send the signal on to the player's synth of choice. The brainchild of Australian player Stevie Chick, this was renamed the Cyberbass in 1994.

Having embraced the five-string bass, the next revolution was to see the instrument lose its head. New York-based Ned Steinberger is the name most readily associated with the configuration, the instruments bearing his name hitting the market in 1981-82. He had designed his first bass, the NS-1, in the mid 1970s for production by Spector; the result in retrospect looks like a prototype Warwick.

The small size of the headless Steinberger's body was compensated for by its construction from graphite, a material that had quite outstanding rigidity for its weight.

BASS-IC MATTERS

(This was the most eye-catching development since Dan Armstrong's experiments with Plexiglas a decade or so before.) As with Ford's Model T, the finish available was "any colour as long as it's black." One of the first players was Andy West of the (Dixie) Dregs, while noted sessioneer Tony Levin bought the first, fretless production model.

The Steinberger player tuned at the opposite end of the guitar than 'conventional' instruments, but this could pose unexpected problems. When he took up the Steinberger in 1981, Bill Wyman got over the problem of where to put his cigarette while playing by gluing the top of a ballpoint pen to the end of the neck – a perfect fit!

There were remarks from players less well-heeled than Wyman on the price of the instrument – a round £1,000, give or take a few pounds. But as Ned Steinberger himself explained in a 1988 magazine article, "it is fabricated from reinforced plastic including, as a major component, carbon fibre one of the most expensive materials on the market, many times the price of even exotic hard wood. We use epoxy resin, also a high-end material, and in every detail the best possible

▲ **Peavey Midibass**

BASS-IC MATTERS

components have been chosen." Add to that three years of research and it was evident why plastic, hitherto used on instruments to be sold cheaply, was out of the price range of many.

Steinberger's lead was followed by

other makers, notably UK manufacturers Status. Their designs by Rob Green attempted to incorporate the best of both worlds, placing wooden 'wings' on to a

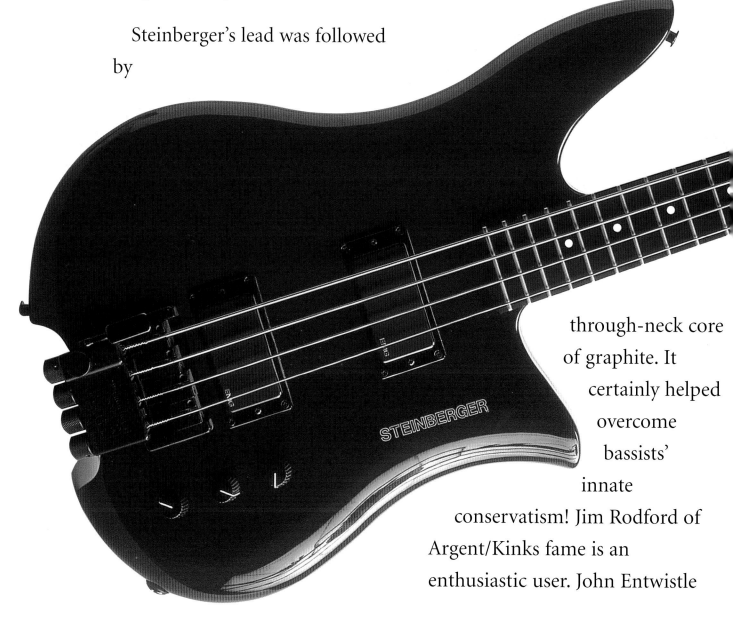

through-neck core of graphite. It certainly helped overcome bassists' innate conservatism! Jim Rodford of Argent/Kinks fame is an enthusiastic user. John Entwistle

▲ Steinberger XM2 Bass

was an enthusiastic user, and had a number of special 'Buzzard' basses made in suitably predatory shapes. (Steinberger eventually capitulated and produced larger-bodied basses, notably the XM2 for Genesis's Mike Rutherford.)

If the

bassist

started life in Leo Fender's words "confined to the back of the band", then the legendary instrument-maker would surely be heartened to see the likes of Flea, with the Red Hot Chili Peppers, proving more of a showman than either of the band's two lead guitarists to date. His style mixes Larry Graham-style slapping with the power of heavy metal, with more than a little punk

attitude thrown in.

The history of the double bass has been traced back to the early 1500s in

Europe. In one tenth of that time, the electric bass guitar has made arguably more of an impact – and certainly produced more star performers. As with so much of the contents of this book, it's all down to Leo Fender.

BASS-IC MATTERS

Postscript: The Chapman Stick

Though not strictly a bass, the Chapman Stick has been taken up by many bass players as an alternative to the conventional bass. The Stick was developed from the guitar and bass, but its playing method shares roots with keyboards and drums, the result being an amazing array of available musical voices.

The idea for the Stick came to American musician Emmett Chapman while playing his guitar in 1969. "No known guitarist, bassist, or fingerboard player had ever before used a basic three and four-fingered technique in each hand simultaneously to play independent lines, scales and chords. It was unique, yet basic and logical – both hands aligned parallel to the frets and perpendicular to the strings, the fingers of each hand fitting sequentially into selected fret spaces at any point along the board."

By 1970 he was playing LA clubs with jazz guitarist Barney Kessel, using this independent hand method to play simultaneous bass, chords and melody on a modified guitar. Later that year he built a body-less version out of an ebony board and called it the Electric Stick, a first production run followed in 1974. Since then many new features have been added to create a variety of related tapping instruments, including eight, 10, and 12-string models. Tony Levin, Nick Beggs and Alphonso Johnson were the first bassists to pick up on the Stick in the late 1970s, and many more have since followed their lead.

Ned Steinberger recently joined forces with Emmett Chapman to create the NS Stick, a hybrid instrument with eight strings designed to be tapped as well as strummed and plucked using conventional techniques. Chapman sees this as an instrument to bridge the gap between the Stick and the guitar/bass. For Steinberger, "The idea with the NS Stick is to be a universal fretboard. That's how I think of it. The idea is for you to decide what you want to do with it. It's set up to pretty much to do it all."

"No known guitarist, bassist, or fingerboard player had ever before used a basic three and four-fingered technique in each hand simultaneously to play independent lines, scales and chords."

MEGA METAL 1980s

The rise of a new generation of heavy metal bands in the 1980s from both sides of the Atlantic seems to have been the driving force behind a plethora of new guitars of various (and often dubious) shapes and sizes. The manufacturer who seemed to best capture the spirit of the age was one BC Rich, whose guitars for a few early 1980s years were a fashion accessory to rival Spandex, headbands and tight T-shirts.

If the Ovation solid-bodies of the 1970s had resembled axe blades, the likes of the Mockingbird and Bich (sic) were more like scythes. In bright colours they were simply vulgar, while the darker-finished versions had an almost gothic appeal, underlined by the company calling a high-range bound Explorer-ish instrument the Warlock.

Rick Derringer, best known or his work with Edgar and Johnny Winter, was an eager BC Rich user, while they even managed to coax Sabbath's Tony Lommi away from his beloved Gibson SG for a spell. Former Runaway Lita Ford enjoyed the guitar's visual appeal, contorting herself with it happily in publicity pictures, while the likes of Blackie Lawless (WASP) and Nikki

▲ BC Rich Mockingbird

Sixx (Mötley Crüe) indulged the less tasteful aspect of angles and colours.

Though an American company, BC Rich manufactured in both the US and Japan. Founder Bernardo Chavo Rico, who gave them their (slightly anglicised) appellation, died in 1999 but his similarly named son, the all-American Bernie, steered the company into the current millennium.

The 1980s was the decade when guitarists were freed from the tyranny of being attached to their effects or amplifiers. UHF wireless systems developed quickly, each requiring little more than a cigar-packet-sized transmitter attached to the belt into which the guitar was plugged for onward transmission of the signal. Teething troubles such as picking

"The 1980s was the decade when guitarists were freed from the tyranny of being attached to their effects or amplifiers."

up local minicab services were overcome and, while the likes of Frank Zappa started the decade as pioneers, the cost of such devices quickly fell so that by the end of the decade 'playing without wires' was within the budget of many more.

Brian May entered the 1980s as the man with the most distinctive

"His guitar was nothing if not original, and was obviously tailored to May's own playing style. 'I like a big neck – thick, flat and wide. I lacquered the fingerboard with Rustin's Plastic Coating.'"

guitar in rock to his name. And, thanks to the huge success of his group Queen, the home-made 'Red Special' he'd made with the help of his dad, Harold, back in the 1960s was known and recognised throughout the world. (From 1984, it has also been built as a replica production guitar by Guild.)

Too broke to buy the Fender Stratocaster hanging in the local music shop, he'd set about building the guitar which would play such a crucial role in the world-famous Queen sound. Having adapted the body of the instrument from the mahogany panelling of an old mahogany fireplace in a friend's house, Brian was soon playing the double-cutaway instrument with its pointy, Flying V-styled headstock in his first pop combo – 1984 – whose repertoire changed as quickly as musical tastes did in the mid-1960s.

But Brian believed his future lay

in the 'heavens', and in 1967 was accepted to study at Imperial College. He kept his hand in with some part-time playing until linking with Roger Taylor in what was to become Queen. His guitar was nothing if not original, and was obviously tailored to May's own playing style. "I like a big neck – thick, flat and wide. I lacquered the fingerboard with Rustin's Plastic Coating." The tremolo was also very interesting, the arm made from an old bicycle saddlebag carrier, the knob at the end from a knitting needle and the springs recycled from an old motorbike. Pickups were scavenged from an old Burns.

As if having such an unique guitar wasn't enough, May insisted on doing things differently at the plucking end. "I use coins instead of a plectrum because they're not flexible. I think you get more control if all the flexing is due to the movement in your fingers. You get better contact with the strings and, depending on how tightly you hold it, you have total control over how hard it's being played. By turning it different ways you can get different sounds, like a slightly grating sound on the beginning of the note…especially when you're using

▲Charvel Surfcaster

193

the guitar at high volume, as I generally do."

Brian's main influence was Jimi Hendrix, who "seemed to push it along so fast in such a short time." In the 1980s, he identified Eddie Van Halen as a similarly important role model. "The kids coming up now who take someone like him as a starting point are going to go a long way. I mean, there was no-one

their bedroom to play with themselves…and come out ready to rock. As the 1980s approached, that man was Van Halen.

On the basis of his band's eponymous debut album, released in April, lead singer David Lee Roth was moved to state: "Eddie Van Halen is the first guitar hero of the 1980s; all the other guitar heroes are dead." Guitar World

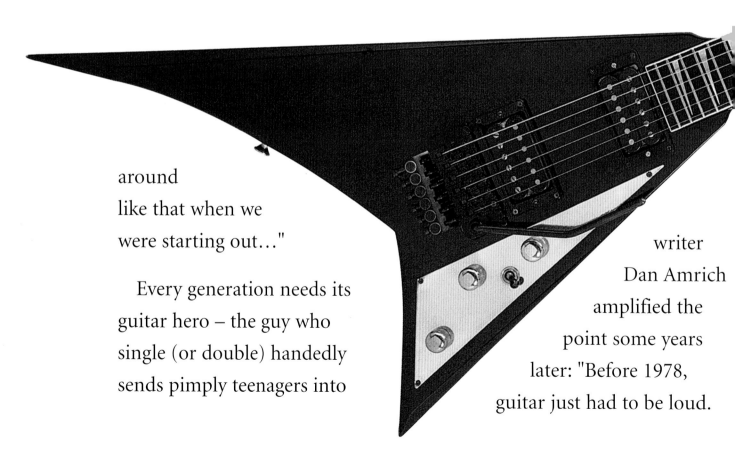

around
like that when we
were starting out…"

Every generation needs its guitar hero – the guy who single (or double) handedly sends pimply teenagers into

writer
Dan Amrich
amplified the
point some years
later: "Before 1978,
guitar just had to be loud.

▲ Jackson Randy Roads

After Van Halen arrived it had to be loud and fast."

Dutch-born brothers Alex and Eddie Van Halen, playing guitar and drums respectively, had swopped instruments early on after starting off playing each other's. "Alex got better than I did – he could play 'Wipeout' and I couldn't – so I bought a guitar."

The scene was certainly ripe for a shakeup as Van Halen made an impact opening for Carlos Santana, UFO and Sparks on the Los Angeles gig circuit. The Claptons, Becks and Pages had either blanded out or semi-retired; acts like Deep Purple and Free were running through doomed six-stringers with depressing speed, while the Allman Brothers and Lynyrd Skynyrd were hobbled by infighting and injury.

Eddie's sound and style came courtesy of a home-made guitar he'd fashioned from $130 worth of spare parts and known as 'Godzilla', its body and neck purchased from Charvel. His first 'name' instrument had been a 1958 Fender Stratocaster – the kind of guitar his idol, Eric Clapton, preferred – but band members felt its single-coil pickups didn't give him a meaty enough sound to power an instrumental three-piece. (Significantly, Clapton had

MEGA METAL 1980s

favoured Gibsons, with their humbucking pick-ups, while with Cream.)

Eddie then went the Gibson route himself with a semi-acoustic ES-335, which gave him something nearer the sound required but failed on image grounds. Besides, Eddie soon found he was missing the Strat's 'whammy-bar', the means by which he achieved a primal effect that would become a trademark. So Godzilla it was…and with a single humbucking pickup near the bridge and just one knob, a volume control, the instrument was simplicity itself.

Decorated with Schwinn bicycle paint in a much-imitated red and white criss-cross pattern, it was the means by which Eddie obtained what he termed his "brown sound – big, warm and majestic". His father Jan was a saxophone player, and Eddie's since suggested he was trying to create a horn-like tone. "If you can get a real, sweet distortion to it, you can make it sound like a sax."

Eddie used that home-made, Charvel-based axe extensively on the first

▲ Gibson ES-335

album (it made a deserved appearance on the cover) and on the road, while his other studio guitar on the sessions was an Ibanez Destroyer similar to those endorsed by Kiss. He plugged into a 100-watt Marshall Super Lead amp that dated from 1967 and was completely unmodified, unlike his guitars, while flange and phase effects, where used, were operated by a footswitch as on stage – a practice that would give current producers apoplexy.

'Van Halen's second track, 'Eruption' was one minute and 42 seconds of pure technical ecstasy. Many people thought the tapping section at the end was a keyboard – but, instead of the left hand fretting strings and the right plucking them, as in conventional playing, both hands are employed on the fretboard simultaneously. Eddie combined pull-offs from the fretboard using the left hand with tapping of the strings with the index finger of the right hand, creating lightning-fast triplet patterns. Such innovatory playing helped him to the title of Best Rock Guitarist in 1979 by readers of Guitar Player magazine, a fifth successive win in 1983 ensuring he was elevated to the

▲ Ibanez Universe

197

Gallery of the Greats.

Van Halen and Dave Lee Roth went their separate ways in 1985, Diamond Dave's replacement, Sammy Hagar, enduring for a decade before a second singer took a walk. By that time, Van Halen had moved on to a different kind of guitar, a Kramer loaded with Gibson pickups. It also had a support behind it which enabled Eddie to swing it out and play it horizontally like a piano to facilitate his tapping technique.

Charvel, whose replacement parts had played such a role in getting Eddie Van Halen off the ground, would soon start marketing complete guitars. By this time Wayne Charvel, who had started the company as purely a component and kit manufacturer, had handed over control to a former employee Grover Jackson. When Jackson started manufacturing under his own name, the Charvel marque was reserved for cheaper, Strat-styled instruments with pointy headstocks and, often, humbucking pickup options.

A few distinctively different guitars would emerge in-

▲ Kramer DMZ Series

between the bread and butter production models, including the Charvel Surfcaster in the early 1990s which took its cues from the Danelectro guitars of the 1960s in its bright colours and lipstick-style pickup covers.

Jackson, meanwhile, focused on the higher-profile end of the metal market – and hooked a rising star in the shape of Randy Rhoads. The outstanding young guitarist, soon to link with Ozzy Osbourne and, tragically, die when an on-the-road prank went wrong, linked with Grover Jackson in 1980 and was heavily involved in the design of the Flying V-derived Jackson Randy Rhoads.

The Soloist, introduced in 1983, was one of the best and most popular examples of the Superstrat – a generic name suggesting its Fender derivation that would cover a large percentage of 1980s designs from all manufacturers. These had pointed headstocks, a locking Floyd Rose-style tremolo and a double-coil (bridge)/single-coil (neck) pickup configuration. respected players like Britain's Paul Samson made these their workhorse. In 1997, Japan's Arai (makers of the Aria range) acquired Jackson/Charvel, leading to the retirement of the

▲ Ibanez "Joe Satriani"
Signature Series

MEGA METAL 1980s

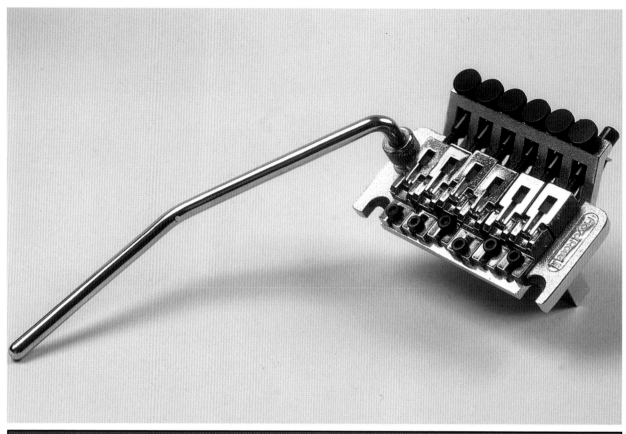

latter name but a continued future for the company.

Just as the Bigsby vibrato unit (tremolo arm to most of us) was the industry standard when it came to third-party guitar hardware in the 1960s and 1970s, so Floyd Rose would become Bigsby's 1980s counterpart. And again it was Eddie Van Halen who

was to blame. In 1981, Kramer had begun a highly significant working relationship with guitarist/machinist Floyd Rose who had been working on the design of a double-locking tremolo unit for several years. Kramer saw the potential in this new device and, with the endorsement of Van Halen, dropped their German-made Rockingers in favour of the new unit in late 1982.

The Floyd Rose allowed upward as well as downward movement – essential for Van Halen – and, pivoting on two large screws in the face of the guitar body, was claimed to stay in tune even after the most excessive abuse. Unusually, the ball at the end of the string had to be cut, each string being held in place by a vice-like clamping assembly within each of the saddles. Its fine tuners were on the top of the unit, just beyond where the hand would rest on the tremolo to mute the strings, and thus offered easy access.

(The major alternative to the Floyd Rose was the Kahler trem, patented in 1984 and invented by David Storey. This pivoted on a ball bearing rather than the Floyd Rose's twin 'knife edge' bearings, but lacked its rival's fine tuners.)

Van Halen's Baretta model guitar, marketed with one slanted humbucker and a single volume control, established Kramer as the biggest star in the 1980s electric guitar firmament. It also introduced the famous 'banana' headstock which became a recognition point until the end of 1986 when a pointed headstock was introduced.

The Fender-

▲ Parker Fly Guitar

esque Pacer – with the archetypal Superstrat humbucker at the bridge in addition to two single-coils – was joined by the Stagemaster arch-top with its through-neck design, including a Paul Dean signature version built for a member of then-popular Canadians Loverboy. (One of Kramer's press ads of the time had guitar-equipped Dean and Van Halen 'dukin' it out' in the boxing ring!)

By 1987 Kramer was the top American guitar producer in sales terms, the Baretta being joined by signature instruments in the Artist series for Elliott Easton (Cars), Richie Sambora (Bon Jovi)

and Vivian Campbell (Dio, later Def Leppard). They also handled Spector guitars and basses, designed by up-and-coming New Yorker Stuart Spector. Next up in 1988 was the Floyd Rose Sustainer, a Strat-style twin humbucker whose neck pickup was designed by Floyd and, at the flip of a switch, would sustain a note for as long as the battery stayed charged – effectively a built-in EBow (see later in this chapter).

The ProAxe and Showster Series were introduced in 1989, the former debuting the newly designed Floyd Rose Pro recessed tremolo system claimed to produce smoother

▲ Gibson Nighthawk

sustain. (This was only offered on the ProAxe.) The Showster had a metal element to its body claimed to produce a better sustaining guitar. Finally in this bewildering array, Kramer began offering their Barettas with Samson wireless systems built in to the guitar itself.

But the ambitious company had seemingly over-extended itself, and bankruptcy resulted. In 1996, Kramer was acquired by Gibson, through a spin-off company, Vaccaro Guitars (founded by Henry Vaccaro, a financial backer of Kramer) they attempted to carry on the aluminium neck tradition the company had forged in the 1970s. Lenny Kravitz and Kid Rock were among early users.

The names of Eddie Van Halen and Steve Vai often go together if only because Vai succeeded EVH as guitarist at the right hand of Dave Lee Roth when he split to go solo. Prior to that, he had spent a spell in Alkatrazz as successor to Yngwie Malmsteen, having made his recording debut in 1981 on Frank Zappa's 'Tinseltown Revolution'.

But if he began from a standing start, Vai soon established himself as not only a guitarist to watch but one who spawned an armoury of

"In 1996, Kramer was acquired by Gibson, through a spin-off company, Vaccaro Guitars..."

203

instruments. He threw in his lot early on with Ibanez, the Japanese manufacturer hitherto best known for their sturdy, workmanlike Gibson copies outlined in chapter six. If they were ready to branch out in more imaginative directions, they had an up and coming guide.

In 1986, Ibanez launched the JEM range of guitars, with Vai (previously a Jackson/BC Rich customer) their major endorsee. A Strat-like body shape and 'pointy' headstock were recognition features, though the major distinguishing mark was a scolloped crescent-moon carrying handle or 'monkey grip'. The Universe, which appeared in 1989, was a seven-stringed instrument with an extra low B; Vai chose an alder-bodied version of this as his main guitar and played it on the Whitesnake album 'Slip Of The Tongue'.

Joe Satriani whose 1987 album, 'Surfing With The Alien' brought guitar instrumental music into the mainstream, vied with Vai in being one of the most influential guitarists of his era. Ironically, they had been schoolmates and he had given Vai his first lessons back in 1973. He too selected an Ibanez guitar as his weapon of choice, creating the Joe Satriani Signature Series

The series boasted necks with hand-polished frets, the fingerboard edges rounded enough to make it feel like a well played-in guitar, while the smooth neck heel allowed good access to the upper frets. "Prestige necks will give you that feeling of unequalled comfort, control and playability, no matter what style of music you play," said

'Satch'. "It's all in the details. These necks feel like they were finished for your very own hands!"

By the 1980s, Gibson's stock had sunk to an all-time low, the company having fallen way behind Fender in the volume guitar stakes (Ibanez and Jackson/Charvel were also major contenders). Ideas like 1980's Sonex 180, with its plastic and wooden core body, was either too far ahead of its time (bearing in mind the Parker Fly) or a desperate shot in the dark that provided an item with a catalogue life of a few brief years.

Very little of note had emerged from their design studio for a number of years, and 1984 saw their parent company, Norlin, close the famed Kalamazoo factory. concentrating production solely in Nashville. A number of ex-employees seized the chance to form their own company with the suitable name of Heritage, and this turned out guitars in familiar ES-175, ES-335 and Les Paul shapes without making a major mark.

Gibson's Nashville plant had been built in 1974 specifically for the production of Les Paul guitars. With few new ideas of note, they tapped their rich history and reissued the dot-neck version of the

▲ Fender Bullet

ES-335 in 1981 and the flametop sunburst Les Paul in 1982. At the same time, the evergreen BB King came on board with his Lucille signature model.

But this would not be enough to save the financially troubled company. Put up for sale at a reported $5 million, it was rescued in January 1986 by Harvard Business School graduates Henry Juszkiewicz, Gary Zebrowski and David Berryman, and the new owners quickly set about the mountainous task of restoring Gibson's reputation for quality as well as its profitability. In 1994, Gibson's Centennial year, the Nighthawk model won an industry award for design, suggesting a new dawn might be near.

The use of effects came to the fore in the 1980s as guitarists like U2's The Edge (real name Dave Evans) made them a trademark of their sound. Their debut album, 'Boy', had showed the footprint of the Electro-Harmonix Memory Man echo unit, an effect that in Edge's words "added seasoning to the soup…we became aware of all these different flavours in our music we hadn't known existed."

Though known as a Stratocaster player, Edge used a Gibson Explorer almost exclusively in the

▲ Tokai Talbo-Tele

band's early Dublin days through a 50-watt Marshall combo – just like Eric Clapton!

The Edge was also a proponent of the hand-held EBow, a small battery-powered device held in the picking hand. Its electrical charge set up an energy field that vibrated the string to produce a powerful sustain, rich in harmonics. This offered the possibility of mimicking horns, synths and woodwinds, or combining with effects to produce outlandish sounds.

Playing the EBow directly over the pickup increased volume and gave the crisp sound of super hot pickups. – "like amplifier feedback with greater control and predictability" – while moving away from the pickup gave a more mellow sound. Invented by Greg

Heet and introduced in 1976, it wasn't quite the most revolutionary development in guitar technology since Leo Fender electrified the instrument in 1948. But it was fun.

Fender had another crack at the lower end of the market in 1981 when they marketed the Bullet series under the slogan "Part Tele. Part Strat. All Excitement." The range to which they were referring, the Bullet, was initially assembled in the States from parts made in Korea – the cost saving being passed on to the customer – but this, Fender's first attempt at manufacturing in the Far East, proved a flop. The Bullet would, however, resurface as part of the Squier budget series.

The effect of mainly Japanese-built copies of classic guitar

▲ Epiphone Supernova

▲ Epiphone Riviera

designs had grown exponentially during the 1970s, as players discovered they could buy something often the equal of a 'real' Strat, Tele or Les Paul at a fraction of the price. The US dollar rose in stature compared with the yen, exacerbating the situation further from the point of view of the American manufacturers or improving the lot of the cash-strapped guitarist depending on which way you looked at it.

Some of the copies would turn out to be superior to their inspirations – and that was certainly the case with Tokai, whose guitars first arrived in Europe in 1981. But they went one step too far by applying suspiciously familiar logos to the headstocks of their guitars, which landed them in legal hot water (their often overlooked original designs included the Talbo – TOkai ALuminium BOdy).

The old maxim 'if you can't beat 'em, join 'em' would soon prove its worth as firstly Fender and then Gibson decided that, if there were going to be Oriental copies of their designs then they were damn well going to do the job themselves.

The Squier company, bought by Fender back in the 1960s, had

▲ Roland GR300

enjoyed a history of over half a century (as evidenced by the 'since 1890' strapline to their logo). Henceforth, though, it would be used to distinguish Japanese-made Strats from Fender's American-manufactured items. Early Squiers had a regular Fender transfer on the headstock, with a smaller 'Squier series' on the rounded end, but this would change to a larger Squier name with 'by Fender' attached.

The early 1980s had seen CBS install a new management team. headed by new president William Schultz. In 1982, the company returned to Leo Fender's original Strat headstock shapes and began making vintage reissues based exactly on the original specifications, while Schultz embarked on a much needed but belated factory modernisation programme. Yet profits were still dropping fast and 1983 saw Fender go down the dangerous road of making economies on their US-manufactured instruments: for instance the loss of the teardrop-shaped chrome jack installation and a tone knob on a Standard Strat and the through-body stringing of the Telecaster.

These cheapskate ideas only lasted a couple of years. Conversely, Elite Series Strats and Teles were marketed that, in the former case, saw push buttons replace the time-honoured pickup selector switch. These sacrilegious 'improvements' proved equally short-lived, though, as with all limited edition guitars, they would command good prices on the vintage market for their rarity value alone.

MEGA METAL 1980s

In 1985, with employment at the Fullerton factory having fallen from a high of 1,100 to just 90 people, CBS sold Fender's name and distribution for $12.5 million to a group of investors headed by Schultz. The company went back to its home-built roots with the American Standard Stratocaster and then Telecaster, built a factory in Corona, California, and began to rebuild its reputation. As the new plant increased in capacity, exchange rates started to favour American-made guitars. Fender was on its way back.

Gibson's Squier equivalent was Epiphone, the company they'd bought in the late 1950s and whose semi-acoustics the Beatles had played in their

▲ Roland GR700

heyday. It took them time to warm to the concept of Oriental production, but by the late 1990s almost every major Gibson marque

was available in a cheaper Epiphone equivalent.

In an echo of their halcyon days, Epiphone came up with some signature variations on their semi-acoustic theme as the millennium turned. Oasis's Noel Gallagher endorsed a Sheraton that was dubbed the Supernova after an Oasis song title, while John Lee Hooker (who died in 2001) and

Jorma Kaukonen put their names to a Sheraton and Riviera respectively.

The 1980s was the decade when the synthesiser appeared to challenge the guitar's traditional domination of the popular music market. Cheap keyboards were inspiring the new generation of musicians, so some guitar manufacturers adopted an 'if you can't beat 'em, join 'em' policy and attempted to merge the two in an attempt to stem the tide. But it wouldn't prove easy…or cheap.

When a keyboard controls a synthesiser of the most basic type, the keys operate as a series of on/off switches. Looked at it in that light, it is surprising anyone ever suggested a guitar could be used to trigger a synth, let alone anything which required touch sensitivity. Roland were first to enter the field with the GR300, which offered six-voice polyphony – but at a price. Players had to pick the strings as cleanly as possible to obtain the desired results: buzzes, squeaks or nay kind of trickery would play havoc with the 'tracking'.

The introduction of the GR700 system in the mid 1980s was a leap forward. The instrument was both unorthodox and distinctive, with a polycarbon bar attaching the headstock to the body, claiming to eradicate harmonic inconsistencies. At the flick of a switch, the G-707 controller could change from a synthesiser controller to a 'conventional' guitar, via the two Les Paul-style humbuckers.

A time lapse between plucking the note and it emerging from the synthesiser was inevitable. But the effectiveness of the synthesiser function can be illustrated by Brian May's solo on Queen's single 'I Want To Break Free'. And even if the system didn't quite let the guitarist do that, it was a

▲ Roland G-707

valiant try.

The SynthAxe was an arrestingly-shaped guitar-style MIDI controller used by jazz guitarists Al Di Meola and Allan Holdsworth and put on the market in 1986 at a price of nearly £10,000 for the complete system.

The SynthAxe's strings were scanned by a microprocessor and the information obtained combined with more from string-bend sensors to determine the pitch of the note. The sensors worked by passing a current through each string and measuring the change of electromagnetic field using small, very delicate coils. As the thickness and tension of the strings had no effect on the pitch, the SynthAxe was strung with 0.13 gauge strings all the way across, giving a very light action.

Trigger keys could also be used which were velocity-sensitive with a polyphonic aftertouch. Once triggered, the fretted string could be let go and the note would sustain until the key was released. That was the theory, at least – equipment crashes were a hazard of the job.

Not quite as futuristic in appearance as the SynthAxe but nevertheless worthy of mention was the Bond Electraglide six-string. It was the brainchild of one Andrew Bond, a luthier from Bournemouth who came to the conclusion, after years of study, that wood was not the optimum material from which to make a guitar. The result of his researches, funded in part by the management of chart stars the Eurythmics, was a carbon-fibre-bodied double cutaway instrument with a phenolic or plastic fingerboard. The latter could be unscrewed and replaced rather than undergoing the conventional re-fret if wear ever became apparent.

Other innovations included a digital display showing the player his current volume and tone settings at a glance – invaluable

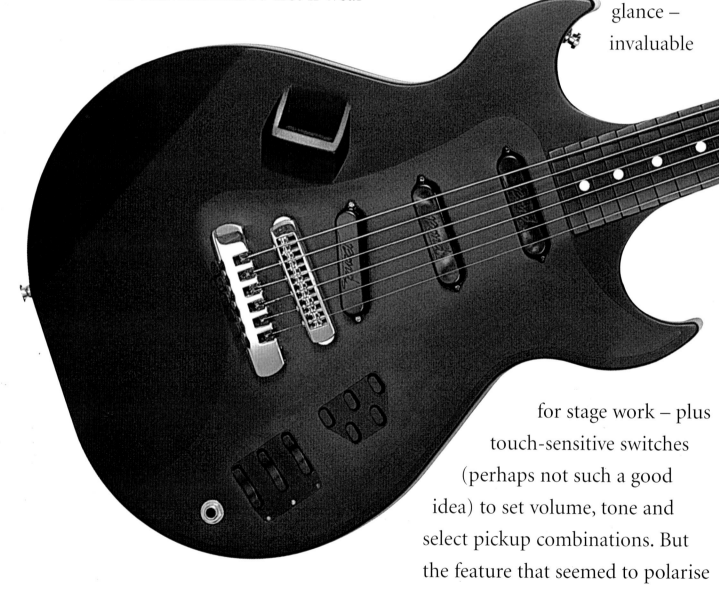

for stage work – plus touch-sensitive switches (perhaps not such a good idea) to set volume, tone and select pickup combinations. But the feature that seemed to polarise

▲ Bond Electraglide 6 String

people was the fat that the fingerboard took a step down after each fret, the 'pitchboard' as it was known then curving up to the next one.

remained a high-priced custom item.

This did not receive universal acceptance, and only just under 1,500 copies of the instrument had emerged from the production line before Bond went belly-up in 1985. Former Clash man Mick Jones, now of hi-tech rockers Big Audio Dynamite, was a convert from his regular Les Paul, while Eurythmic Dave Stewart showed loyalty by giving it a try, but most Bonds nowadays reside in collections – a production guitar that arguably should have

The 1980s had spawned a number of heroic failures and unusual shapes as well as the ubiquitous Superstrat pack. But with both Gibson and Fender under new management, a revival of traditional values seemed likely in the coming decade.

FUTURISTIC 1990s

▲ PRS Custom

▲ PRS Santana III

If the 1980s had seen high performance guitars hit the headlines, the trend in the 1990s was to rediscover some of the old virtues. Floyd Rose trems had acquired the sobriquet in some quarters of 'sustain drains', and when Slash, lead guitarist of happening heavy metal band Guns N'Roses adopted a classic, hardtail Les Paul sunburst rather than some pointy-headed, vibrato-equipped Superstrat it appeared to confirm a new (or maybe the return of an old) order.

The biggest new name on the scene by far was Paul Reed Smith, an American guitar maker who sought to embody the classic Les Paul virtues in a new design. The PRS Custom appeared in 1985 and appeared to combine Les Paul sonics in its arched, figured maple top with a double-cutaway nod to the Strat. Also Strat-like was a five-way pickup option (though accessed via a rotary switch) allowing the PRS-manufactured humbuckers to offer both humbucking and single-coil sounds.

Rick Derringer, for one, was convinced. "These guitars are the perfect mix of a Strat and Les Paul," he enthused, "the combination of a glued-in maple neck, three single-coil soapbar pickups, five-way blade selector switch, two-point fulcrum vibrato and Gibson scale make these guitars go from rock to jazz in an instant."

Gibson's attempt to follow suit in 1993 with the Nighthawk, combining a Les Paul shape with Strattish controls, did less well. Though it won an industry award for design and was said by one impressed guitar-maker to be "the best guitar Gibson has made in 25 years", it stayed in production a matter of a few years and was discontinued in 1999. It appeared the ever-conservative guitarist expected a Gibson to be…well, a Gibson.

But back to Paul Reed Smith, a man who "has done more for the high end guitar market than any other person alive." Those are the words of American luthier Ed Roman, who continues: "The absolute best thing that Paul ever did was to bring the perceived price of an electric guitar up to the level where a consumer would actually consider buying a custom-made instrument. Today there are hundreds of small builders who owe their success to Paul. I am one of them."

Paul Reed Smith certainly swam against the tide of Oriental copies that had dented the guitar market in volume terms for the past two decades. Smith succeeded where others failed by sheer determination. Having sold early custom guitars to Ted Nugent and Peter Frampton, his next ambition was to make an instrument for his all-time musical hero, Carlos Santana. Having got backstage with an instrument in 1976, he caught the great man's ear, but Santana

▲ Gibson Nighthawk

was involved with Yamaha. Four years later, Smith tried again, and this time Carlos took his guitar on stage. He didn't get on with the P90-style pickups but was otherwise pleased enough to order a humbucker-equipped flame-top model – only the third PRS had made – with a vibrato, which Smith had never yet done.

The instrument was complete within a month, and was followed by another model with a tone control (Santana settled on one volume, one tone and a three-way pickup selector), then a third with Seymour Duncan Custom and '59 pickups. It was now a question of whether PRS would stay a small operation or build guitars for a wider market. The answer came in 1985 when Smith began limited hand-made production of the PRS Custom. His finishes were the best

"The answer came in 1985 when Smith began limited hand-made production of the PRS Custom. His finishes were the best in the industry, while items like the locking tuning pegs have since been widely copied."

FUTURISTIC 1990s

in the industry, while items like the locking tuning pegs have since been widely copied. PRS used only the finest Brazilian rosewood for his fingerboards and the wood used for the bodies and necks were tone woods that they had "hoarded and

stashed for years". These were vintage guitars right off the production line.

In 1995 PRS expanded their factory and, for a year, demand for

the products greatly exceeded supply. A situation arose similar to that of Fender pre-and post the 1965 takeover by CBS, guitarists

▲ PRS Tremonti

perceiving a drop in quality (whether real or imagined). Many people who bought PRS instruments in 1993 were able to sell them in later years for more than double what they paid in 1996.

But PRS guitars had never been intended for the investment market and by introducing the Santana III and Tremonti guitars (the latter a signature model of Mark Tremonti, guitarist with Creed) they ensured there was still the possibility of less than mega-rich players achieving the dream. This may or may not have pleased the likes of Ed Roman, but it made sense. On the other side of things, a Private Stock operation still existed for the well-heeled, with Paul himself personally checking each instrument before delivery. Like the distinctive bird-shaped mother of pearl inlays in the fretboards of his top-level guitars, Paul Reed Smith is still flying high.

Peter Frampton was the first customer for Smith's solid-body designs, Ted Nugent having opted for a semi. The choice of artist had been because Paul Reed Smith had grown up on an older brother's record collection which included Frampton's work with Humble Pie.

And who, living through the 1970s, could not have been touched by 'Frampton Comes Alive', an album so ubiquitous comedy actor Mike Myers (of Wayne's World fame) claimed it "came along with the soap powder"?

The gatefold sleeve showed Frampton playing a black three-pickup Les Paul dating from 1954, and in 2002 he admitted to this writer that he had never fully got over its loss in a cargo plane crash in South America in 1980. "I lost the Les Paul, but three people died so I can't whine too much about that.

"But then about four years ago I was living in Nashville, where Gibson is based. I would slip out the back door, jump in the car and go and have coffee with the guys there, hang out. One thing led to another, the head of Gibson said 'Isn't it about time we had a Peter Frampton model?' and I said 'I thought you'd never ask!' So we spent a year with the custom shop there with Mike McGuire, and spent as much time as I wanted working on it.

"Because most Pauls are so heavy these days and we're not allowed to use Honduras mahogany – which is the lightest mahogany – for preservation / conservation reasons they have to use other mahogany which is just godawful heavy, he decided to do some sound chambers in it. I wasn't sure, but he had a go and it ended up sounding so much like my original one because it was lighter I guess.

"My original was a 'Black Beauty' converted from a 1954

body that someone had found, turned and routed, so we decided to give this new one a little more top and treble. I went with a maple top, so it does have a veneer of maple on the top whereas a normal '57 Les Paul Custom is totally mahogany.

"Wiring-wise, I never liked the way they wired those three-pickup guitars because you could never get each pickup on individually. This one is wired like a regular two-pickup, except both pickups are wired to the top volume and tone, but you still use the switch; the bottom volume and tone are purely

for the centre pickup, so you dial it in when you need it. That gives you a regular Les Paul with an added bonus."

Even the venerable Stratocaster was on its way back, and a new chapter of the Strat's history was about to be written under the company's post-CBS management. In 1990 Fender published a single-spaced index that included 31 different Stratocasters on the first page alone, while the 1992 catalogue pictured 44 variations on the classic theme.

Players failing to find production models fitting their needs could consider a top-of-the-line guitar from the Fender Custom

▲ Parker Fly Guitar

Shop.

The Strat continued to be associated with a host of major players: Eric Clapton, Jeff Beck, Bonnie Raitt, Robert Cray, David Gilmour and Mark Knopfler were still on the scene, while Smashing Pumpkins leader Billy Corgan was among the new breed. Raitt became the first woman – possibly in guitar history – to have a signature model guitar, donating the proceeds to a scheme helping inner-city girls pursue careers in music.

Shadow-in-chief Hank Marvin was certainly convinced that Fender were back.

"I think they turned the corner when they bought the factory back from CBS and started producing some quality instruments," he said in 2003. "I think Fender make some fab instruments now and I've been impressed by every one of them I've been given to try. I wish guitars like this had been available when we all started in 1957, whenever it was, with this quality of fingerboard and action at this sort of price. A lot of the guitars about then had high actions, rough frets, things like that."

The Strat, then, remained the most recognisable silhouette in the electric guitar

▲ Musicman Silhouette

world. When it came to revolutionary shapes, there were few to rival the Parker Fly. It is constructed of wood, the back of which is reinforced with a high modulus carbon and glassfibre fabric, the whole baked under pressure to form a rigid, resonant body structure. This allows for a very thin and extremely lightweight guitar. Each guitar is fitted with both DiMarzio electric (humbucking) pickups and Piezo transducers in the bridge, stereo outputs allowing the player to send the 'acoustic' sound to the PA system and the electric to his stage amp.

Founded by Ken Parker and Larry Fishman, Parker Guitars delivered its first production Fly from its Wilmington, Massachusetts factory in July 1993, after two years of development.

Since then, Parker has shipped thousands of instruments worldwide, introduced several more models and provided musicians with a guitar arguably more diverse than any other on the market.

"The Fly exceeded my wildest dreams," recounted co-founder Ken Parker. "I started toying with the idea of the Fly in the 1980s and when we finally shipped the first one I really didn't know what to expect. But the response turned out to be incredible. Musicians from every genre of music have told me unique and personal reasons why they love their Fly."

Parker players in the high-profile rock world include Dave Navarro (of Jane's Addiction/Red Hot Chili Peppers), Joe Walsh (Eagles), Reeves Gabrels (Bowie) and Mark

Farner (Grand Funk Railroad), but the likes of Merle Haggard and Joni Mitchell have also invested. In 1996, American Christian musician Phil Keaggy recorded an entire album, the punningly titled 'On The Fly', with the instrument, while Aerosmith's Tom Hamilton was one of the first users of the Fly Bass.

The Fly Classic and Fly Deluxe models were revised to celebrate the design's tenth birthday, while the newly introduced Parker Mojo was designed specifically to get "that crunchy, heavy rock tone." But not everyone was convinced: EMG pickups supremo Rob Turner has gone on record as saying that "unless Jimi Hendrix comes back to life" and plays a Parker he doubts it will bridge the gap and become a ubiquitous 'name' guitar.

Music Man, the company launched by Leo Fender and several ex-Fender employees, had perhaps surprisingly gone from strength to strength after being taken over by stringmaker Ernie Ball. The StingRay bass had established itself as a benchmark in the four-string world before the change in management, but the guitar section of the market had remained relatively unimpressed.

This situation was to change in the 1990s, the seeds for the shift having been sown in 1986 with the introduction of the Silhouette. This was in effect a re-interpretation of Leo's perennial Stratocaster theme, but would capture he imagination of a number of leading players who would use it as the basis for their own signature models.

One such was Steve Morse, founder of the Dixie Dregs, who would go on to inherit the lead guitarist berth in Deep Purple when Ritchie Blackmore quit in 1994. He selected Music Man to build his signature model guitar in 1987. Like all the company's designs after the earliest StingRays and Sabres, the four lower strings had their pegs at the top of the headstock, Fender-fashion, the highest two protruding below to give a not unattractive asymmetrical effect.

Britain's Albert Lee adopted a prototype instrument, made in 1987, and featuring a radical angular body as his own. In 1993 Ernie Ball offered this guitar to the public as the Albert Lee Signature model with a 'pinkburst' finish, three Seymour Duncan single coils, a maple neck and a Music Man standard (non-tremolo) bridge.

Also introduced in 1993 was the Luke, signature instrument of Toto's Steve Lukather. The instrument featured one (bridge) and two single-coil EMG active pickups. A Music Man Floyd Rose licensed locking tremolo and a vintage 'deep-V' profile neck completed the package.

But by far the

▲ Musicman "Albert Lee" Signature Model

biggest endorsee was one Edward Van Halen, who lent his name to the EVH from January 1990 to late 1995 (after which it reverted to being the Axis). Press ads at the time rammed home his involvement with the strapline: "I endorsed the guitar I used to play. I designed this one. Big difference." The Axis featured a bass-wood body with a bound, book-matched figured maple top and a digitally carved neck. Needless to say, the Axis was available with Music Man's Floyd Rose trem.

The 1986-vintage Silhouette was basically the production model of the Steve Morse signature guitar and was rare among modern designs in becoming part of the armoury of Rolling Stones Ronnie Wood and Keith Richards. The Silhouette Special, introduced in 1995, featured patented 'Silent Circuit' electronics, claimed to significantly reduce single-coil hum without altering the instrument's bright, vintage sound. A strategy of continuous refinement is likely to keep Music Man at the forefront of guitar manufacture for some while to come.

Highly rated British luthier Patrick Eggle's early 1990s Berlin design looked not

▲ **Musicman EVH**

dissimilar in layout to a Paul Reed Smith. But unlike his US counterpart, he would spend the decade joining forces with other makers and distributors in an effort to bridge the gap between custom building and mass-market musical instruments.

Patrick graduated from the London College of Furniture and, with the financial help of the Prince's Trust, quickly managed to impress many famous British musicians like Brian May (Queen), Toni Lommi (Black Sabbath), Midge Ure (Ultravox), Nik Kershaw and Noel Gallagher (Oasis) with his well made guitars. The Berlin Pro, reminiscent of a PRS design, remains the top-rated Eggle guitar today, while the more affordable New York combined a maple/alder body with a Superstrat-style pickup

arrangement. The semi-hollow New York Broadway had a mahogany back and coil-tappable Seymour Duncan pickups which enabled the player to switch from a Rickenbacker-type jangle to a weightier Gibson ES-335 impersonation.

One of the manufacturers Eggle had linked with was Gary Levinson whose Blade guitar was a refinement of the tried and trusted Strat. Levinson had begun repairing guitars in 1964 and, having multiple university degrees in applied and natural sciences, approached guitar building from an analytical standpoint. Inherent resonant frequencies of woods, innovative electronics and the tonal effect of hardware were all important factors in his approach to instrument development.

"The wonderful thing about repair work," he's said, "is that you learn what is troubling guitarists and what they really would like their instrument to give them in regard to features, feel and playability. The Blade was the result of more than 20 years of solving the problems that guitarists brought me. Every piece of technology was developed to meet a specific need that the musicians had expressed to me."

In 1982 he built a series of Blade prototypes utilising innovative pickups but it took fully five years to forge the links with manufacturing partners that enabled the Blade to be launched on a world-wide scale. By 1990 the Swiss-manufactured Blade had become the best selling 'high-end' custom guitar in Europe and received endorsements from many notable players. These included Phil Manzanera (Roxy Music), Steve Rothery (Marillion) and John Ellis (Stranglers).

The current range of Levinson guitars is standardised around the Texas (Strat) and Delta (Tele) style designs, along with the Jazz Bass inspired Tetra and (five string) Penta, all built on the concept of "Classic Design, Creative Technology". Guitar Player magazine, for one, approved. "While most companies grind out clones, a few pioneering souls dedicate themselves to building instruments for the next decade. Take Gary Levinson, one of the world's truly innovative electric guitar designers..."

From the sublime to the arguably ridiculous, even lower-priced guitar-makers were getting in on the 'signature' act. Kiss's Paul Stanley, whose first guitar – like so many other American rockers – was a Silvertone, decided to give that company their first personality-endorsed model. "We wanted to create something that had never been done before – a high quality signature series that everyone can afford," enthused the rejuvenated company. "Paul came into the office for days just to sit at a drafting table and design unique guitars for the coming Kiss tour. Our Custom Shop built the tour models and the prototypes to Paul's specifications. The production

samples have been approved and production will begin immediately on our new high-end production line in Indonesia."

The Apocalypse (in guitar and bass options), Sovereign and Dark Star acoustic were all on catalogue, while a Kiss backstage amp was available for all those who wished to indulge their fantasies in private…

Effects and amplification came together in the 1990s when 'pods' appeared on the market allowing the guitarist to emulate any amp he wished. The Line 6 Pod was designed to 'model' (imitate) a selection of classic

▲ Patrick Eggles Guitar

233

FUTURISTIC 1990s

amplifiers, allowing guitarists amazing flexibility both on stage and in the studio. The concept was an immediate success, and would lead to the Variax guitar which could similarly replicate a variety of well known guitars. There was no doubt that, as the century ended, the guitarist had a bewildering array of possibilities before him (or indeed her) compared with what Scotty Moore and Bill Haley had to contend with.

Grunge was the pre-eminent street-level trend of the 1990s, and

▲ **Fender Jaguar**

Nirvana from Washington were its most successful exponents. The songs combined quiet passages with louder choruses, a fuzzy sound being

preferred. This was sometimes obtained by the use of preamplifiers used by grunge players, with a resurgence in the brown sound and good tone to suit blues and rock players.

Nirvana's Kurt Cobain, a left-handed player, complained it wasn't easy to find reasonably priced, high-quality guitars. But, while he was looking, the Fender Mustang had become his unlikely stage favourite because "they're

cheap and totally inefficient, and they sound like crap and are very small." The combination of the Mustang's short scale and heavy strings helped lead to Cobain's signature sound.

When the genre-launching 'Nevermind' was a runaway success he had a queue of custom guitar makers at his door, but linked with Danny Ferrington of the Fender Custom Shop to find him left-handed necks to replace the ones he destroyed on stage. The next stop was to assemble something better.

It combined the body shape and headstock of a Fender Mustang with a Gibson-style Tune-O-Matic bridge and three Bartolini pickups – a humbucker at the bridge with single coils elsewhere, Superstrat-style.

The instrument's body was made of basswood, with a maple neck and rosewood fretboard. The blue body colour and tortoise shell pickguard were Cobain's choices, as were heart-shaped fret inlays.

Cobain's favourite electric guitar of all, which remained safely studio-bound, was a Jaguar. In a now-famous design exercise, he took Polaroid photos of a Mustang and a Jaguar, cut them in half and stuck them together to reveal a guitar with the upper part of the Mustang body and the lower portion of the Jaguar. The result, named the Jagstang, had an alder body, a 24-inch maple neck with a rosewood fretboard and vintage-style fretwire. The neck pickup was a single-coil Fender Texas Special, which was originally designed as a bridge pickup for Fender's Stevie Ray Vaughan model, with a DiMarzio humbucker at the neck.

Kurt requested two guitars, one in Solid Blue and one in Fiesta Red. The blue instrument was used on Nirvana's 1993 tour, while the red guitar, which was about to be delivered on Cobain's death, will be exhibited in the planned Fender Museum. Production models of the Jagstang found favour with the public, but the guitar was only available for a few years.

had failed to do for Fender's sales figures what Hendrix had managed a quarter of a century earlier, he would rightly go down in music history for what he achieved with one – or maybe two – of Leo's timeless creations.

There were, inevitably, echoes of fellow Seattle guitarist Jimi Hendrix in Cobain's sad, sudden demise. Yet while he

▲ Fender Jagstang

So where is the electric guitar headed in the 21st century? It's tempting to leave the page blank, because it's such a difficult question to answer. The innovation of rock'n'roll has, over the years, been tempered by guitar players' innate conservatism in favour of 'name' guitars and known designs. If you doubt this, consider that Sex Pistol Sid Vicious 'played' a Fender Precision Bass!

No less a person than Les Paul has said that "Guitar makers are stuck in the past…making guitars the same as those made all those years ago." It's a hard accusation to refute – but should they be criticised for that? It all depends on where you sit.

Talking to this author on the eve of the Stratocaster's half-century in 2004, Hank Marvin – the first man in Britain to own one – is clearly still besotted with his first love. "The impact, visually, of that guitar…" he sighed, "I know that's not the important thing, it's the sound – well, not just the sound but things like the tremolo arm system, which to me was manna. It just looked so incredible. When we opened the case (in 1959) I remember we just stood looking down at this thing on the floor – it was just out of this world. And when you look at a Strat today it's still a fabulous-looking guitar. It's become a classic. I know people have based concepts on it and gone off on tangents. but they always look like they're not quite as well proportioned, somehow."

Someone who'd agree with the bespectacled Stratmeister is John 'Gypie' Mayo, once of Doctor Feelgood, now of the rejuvenated

Yardbirds. He is still the proud owner of a '62 Strat, his main guitar in Feelgoods' days – and is so happy with it he had it cloned! "About a year after I first joined the Yardbirds, Arbiters gave me a Japanese-built '62 reissue to take to America on our first tour there as it would be less likely to be stolen. All they wanted was a few photos, which they never did ask for! But I was really very pleased to get the guitar 'cause it really does sound and feel like a '62 – others who've played it have agreed. So that's my main stage guitar now."

But he doesn't agree that you can't improve on perfection. Apart from fitting Kluson machine heads, he's installed a Seymour Duncan Hotrails pickup with a coil tap at the bridge. "Seymour Duncan are sorting out the other pickups because I do have noise

"Les Paul has said that 'Guitar makers are stuck in the past…making guitars the same as those made all those years ago.'"

problems from time to time depending on the wiring at the venues. The old single-coil syndrome…" Mayo's amplification set-up is also a 'new for old' affair with a Vox AC30 reissue which he finds "keeps that classic brightness and clarity at low volumes."

Another quintessentially English player, Richard Thompson, has retired his workhorse Stratocasters,

239

a '59 and '66, in favour of a similarly configured, custom-made instrument designed by Danny Ferrington. "It's like a Strat," he remarks, "but with a slightly different body shape. The pickups – a Broadcaster in the bridge, an Alnico Strat pickup in the middle and a Gibson P90 in the neck – interact in an interesting way. It's a testbed guitar and it works well." Never one for excess, Thompson even used a Danelectro eight-inch practice amp in the making of 2003 release 'The Old Kit Bag'.

So what would happen to guitars no longer wanted on voyage? Many – too many – have ended up on the walls of hamburger joints across the globe, and it would be nice if, like the late Rory Gallagher's instruments, there was the chance for young players to enjoy an encounter with music

history. Rory's collection of over 100 guitars will, says his brother Donal, be kept together. "I'm a motor enthusiast, and there's nothing worse than seeing vintage cars in a garage all polished and gleaming when they should be taken out and thrashed. It's like an art collection, and that's the way I want to keep it, but I'd like to see them working as well. There's a location in Ireland that, if it comes right, might be a permanent home. There's a range of amps as well, old Fender Tweeds and stuff, and these things don't last forever. I'd like an environment with a studio where people, young guitar players, could try them out."

The simplicity of Rory's trademark, sweat-worn trademark 1963 Strat was a long way from the brave new worlds promised by the likes of Bond and Parker. The title

THE GUITAR IN THE 21ST CENTURY

of most heroic failure, however, surely belonged to the Yamaha G10, the latest of their guitar synthesiser range which went on sale in 1988. The attraction of its futuristic Steinberger-like shape, matt grey finish and guitar-like neck could not overcome the complexity of operation which required three pickups to register pitch (which fret was being used), pluck (the strength at which the string was hit) and bend (any sideways movement). Since this amazing piece of kit appeared and rapidly disappeared in 1988, the Roland pickup that can be attached to a conventional guitar has remained the best way to drive a MIDI synthesiser from a stringed instrument.

But a big advance was promised with the advent of the digital guitar, brainchild of Gibson chief Henry Juszkiewicz and planned for introduction in 2004. The intention, according to Craig Devin, who worked on the technology, was "to obsolete all guitars…through a technology play." Journey guitarist Neal Schon tested some of Gibson's prototypes and pronounced them "pretty incredible".

Gibson's patented HEX pickup was claimed to sense up-and-down motion (like an acoustic guitar pickup) and side-to-side motion (like an electric guitar pickup) for each string. Most impressive of all was the fact that the digital signal created inside the guitar did not degrade even with 200 feet of cable. The guitars will have two jacks — one for the ethernet cable and one for the old-style analogue lead – and will add about $200 to a $1,000-plus price-tag .

"Moving further into the sonic realm, the digital guitar could assign a different effect to each of the six strings..."

The possibilities seemed endless. The ethernet cable from the guitar could be connected to a digital amp, or to a laptop which could then become a mixing board. Potentially, soundchecks would no longer be necessary. After the guitarist had set up his or her preferences for how the instrument should sound, the laptop could automatically adjust the settings so it sounded exactly right in that particular room. The system could also adjust the sound to the room's changing acoustics as the number of people in the audience increased.

Moving further into the sonic realm, the digital guitar could assign a different effect to each of the six strings, adding hitherto unimagined new capabilities to the instrument, but Neal Schon thought this might be a step too far. "Every guitar player is going to look at (Gibson) like they're from outer space and say, 'I don't need it!' "

Gibson's network system is called MaGIC – Media-accelerated Global Information Carrier – and they hope it will be adopted as an industry standard by amp makers and others. "We set out to do this product and set a standard for the music business," says Gibson's

Juszkiewicz. How successful he will be remains to be seen…

Maybe another, simpler route to the future was visible in the shape of the Variax, manufactured by Pod experts Line 6 and able to reproduce the sound of most 'name' guitars', both acoustic and electric. "Variax isn't just a guitar – it's a revolution," their advertising proclaimed. "With a single beautifully crafted instrument, you'll have instant access to a showroom full of the worlds finest-sounding guitars."

This was obviously a lot handier than carrying around a number of different instruments to use on different numbers (though variations in tuning would still have to be accommodated). The jury is still out on what level of acceptance the guitar will enjoy –

and at around £730 it appeared reasonably priced – but in terms of usefulness it must come high up the list of recent trends. Indeed, Line 6 have extended the concept to the Guitar Port, a device that can be linked to the Internet via a PC and allow guitarists to download new sounds, lessons, effects and even play along with Jimi Hendrix backing tracks.

The combination of the electric guitar and the Internet would seem to connect the old and the new in a fascinating way. Despite the innate conservatism of many of its players, the instrument that had shaped the sound of half a decade of music seemed set to continue its quest for fresh fields to conquer.

PICTURE INDEX

PICTURE INDEX

PICTURE INDEX

PICTURE INDEX

DISCOGRAPHY

It's impossible to do more than scratch the surface, but we have tried to suggest a recommended listening item for a number of the players who appear in the text and/or deserve your attention. Omissions should not be taken personally!

Albert King - Gibson Flying V
'Best Of Albert King Vol 1' (Stax)

Andy Summers - Hamer
Police: 'Very Best Of Sting And The Police' (A&M)

Angus Young - Gibson SG
AC/DC: 'Back In Black' (Atlantic)

BB King- Gibson ES-355 Lucille
'His Definitive Greatest Hits' (Universal TV)

Bill Wyman - Various
The Rolling Stones: '40 Licks' (Rolling Stones/Virgin)

Billy Sheehan - Yamaha BB3000S
Dave Lee Roth: 'Eat 'Em And Smile' (Warner Bothers)

Bootsy Collins - Washburn Space Bass
'Back In the Day: The Best Of' (Warner Brothers)

Buddy Guy - Fender Stratocaster
'Damn Right I Got The Blues' (Silvertone)

Buddy Holly - Fender Stratocaster
'The Very Best Of' (Universal TV)

Carlos Santana - Gibson SG, Paul Reed Smith
'The Ultimate Collection' (Sony)
'Supernatural' (Arista)

Carol Kaye - Fender Stratocaster

Various singles by the Beach Boys, Glen Campbell, Joe Cocker etc

Chris Squire - Rickenbacker 4001S bass

Yes: '90125' (Atlantic)

Chuck Berry - Gibson ES-350

'The Best Of' (MCA)

Cliff Gallup - Gretsch Duo-Jet

Gene Vincent: 'The Best Of Volume 1' (EMI)

Dave Gilmour - Fender Stratocaster

'Echoes: The Best Of Pink Floyd' (EMI/Harvest)

Duane Allman - Gibson SG

'Duane Allman: An Anthology' (Capricorn)

Duane Eddy - Gretsch Chet Atkins

'The Best Of Duane Eddy' (RCA)

Eddie Van Halen - Charvel 'Godzilla'

'Van Halen' (Warner Brothers)

Eric Clapton - Gibson Les Paul, Fender Stratocaster

John Mayall: 'Bluesbreakers Featuring Eric Clapton' 'The Cream Of Eric Clapton' (Polydor)

Frank Zappa

'Shut Up 'N Play Your Guitar' (Barking Pumpkin)

Freddie King - Gibson Les Paul, ES-335

'Hideaway - The Best Of' (Rhino)

DISCOGRAPHY

Geddy Lee - Rickenbacker 4001 bass
Rush: 'Chronicles' (Mercury)

Hank B. Marvin - Fender Stratocaster
The Shadows: '20 Golden Greats' (EMI)

Jack Bruce - Gibson EB-3 bass
Cream: 'Disraeli Gears' (Polydor)

Jaco Pastorius - Fender Fretless Jazz Bass
'Punk Jazz: The Anthology' (Rhino)

James Jamerson - Fender Precision Bass
Many Motown hits

Jeff Beck - Fender Stratocaster
'Beckology' (Epic)

Jimi Hendrix - Fender Stratocaster
'Are You Experienced' (Polydor)

Jimmy Page - Gibson SG-1275, Les Paul
'Led Zeppelin IV' (Atlantic/Swan Song)

Joe Satriani - Ibanez JS-6
'Surfing With The Alien' (Food For Thought)

Joe Walsh - Gibson Les Paul
'Look What I Did: The Anthology' (MCA)

John Entwistle
The Who: 'Who's Next' (Polydor)
The Who: 'Who's Better, Who's Best' (Polydor)

Johnny Marr - Rickenbacker 360
The Smiths - 'The Smiths' (Warner

Brothers)

Johnny Winter - Gibson Firebird
'The Collection' (Castle)

Keith Richards - Fender Telecaster
The Rolling Stones: '40 Licks' (Rolling Stones/Virgin)

Larry Graham - Fender Precision Bass
'The Jam: Anthology' (Rhino)

Marcus Miller - Fender Jazz Bass
Miles Davis: 'The Man With the Horn' (Sony)

Mark Knopfler - Fender Stratocaster
Dire Straits: 'Dire Straits' (Warner Brothers)

Michael Schenker - Gibson Flying V
'Portfolio' (Chrysalis)

Mick Jones - Gibson Les Paul
The Clash - 'The Clash' (Sony)

Mick Ronson - Gibson Les Paul
David Bowie: 'The Rise And Fall Of Ziggy Stardust And The Spiders From Mars' (EMI)

Muddy Waters - Fender Telecaster
'The Best Of' (Chess)

Paul McCartney - Hofner Violin Bass, Rickenbacker 4001S
'All The Best' (EMI)
'The Beatles 1962-66' (Apple)
'The Beatles 1967-70' (Apple)

Paul Weller - Rickenbacker 330
The Jam: 'All Mod Cons' (Polydor)

DISCOGRAPHY

Percy Jones - Wal bass
Brand X: Unorthodox Behaviour'
(Virgin)

Pete Townshend - Rickenbacker 330, Gibson SG
The Who: 'Who's Next' (Polydor)
The Who: 'Who's Better, Who's Best' (Polydor)

Richard Thompson - Fender Stratocaster
Fairport Convention: 'The History Of' (Island)
'Watching The Dark: The Richard Thompson Anthology' (Ryko)

Ritchie Blackmore - Fender Stratocaster
Rainbow: 'Rising' (Polydor)

Robert Cray - Fender Stratocaster
'Strong persuader' (Phonogram)

Robert Fripp - Gibson Les Paul
King Crimson: 'Young Person's Guide To King Crimson' (EG)

Ry Cooder - Various
'Why Don't You Try Me Tonight' (Warner Brothers)

Scott Gorham - Gibson Les Paul
Thin Lizzy: 'Live and Dangerous' (Phonogram)

Scotty Moore - Gibson 400 CES
Elvis Presley: 'The Sun Sessions' (RCA)

Slash - Gibson Les Paul
Guns N'Roses: 'Appetite For Destruction' (Geffen)

Stanley Clarke - Alembic bass
'Hot Fun: The Best Of' (Zounds Music)

Steve Cropper - Fender Telecaster
Booker T and the MGs 'The Best Of' (Stax)

Steve Howe - Gibson E-175
Yes: 'Fragile' (Atlantic)

Steve Vai - Ibanez JEM
'Passion And Warfare' (Food For Thought)

Stevie Ray Vaughan - Fender Stratocaster
'Texas Flood' (Sony)

Sting - Fender Precision Bass
Police: 'Very Best Of Sting And The Police' (A&M)

T-Bone Walker - Gibson ES-5
'The Complete Imperial Recordings 1950-54/Original 1945-50 Performances' (Capitol)

The Edge - Gibson Explorer
U2: 'The Unforgettable Fire' (Island)

Tim Bogert - Fender Precision Bass
Vanilla Fudge: 'Psychedelic Sundae: The Best Of' (Atco)

Verdine White - Ibanez Signature
Earth Wind & Fire: 'The Ultimate Collection' (Sony TV)

Wilko Johnson - Fender Telecaster
Doctor Feelgood: 'Stupidity' (Grand)

BOOK LIST

Inevitably, many a book and magazine, not to mention website, has been consulted in the research for this volume. All publications in the list below are highly recommended as well as acknowledged.

1000 Great Guitarists – Hugh Gregory (Balafon)

50 Years Of Fender – Tony Bacon (Miller Freeman Books)

Bass Book – Tony Bacon & Barry Moorhouse (Balafon)

Bass Heroes (edited Tom Mulhern) (Miller Freeman Books)

Blues Guitar – Jas Obrecht (Miller Freeman Books)

Complete Guitar Guide – David Lawrenson (Virgin Books)

Electric Guitar (edited - Paul Trynka) (Virgin Books)

Electric Guitars - The Illustrated Encyclopedia (Bacon, Burrluck, Day, Wright) (Balafon)

Fender Amp Book – John Morrish (Balafon)

Fender Book – Tony Bacon & Paul Day (Balafon)

Fuzz & Feedback – Tony Bacon (Miller Freeman Books)

Gibson Les Paul Book – Tony Bacon & Paul Day (Balafon)

Gretsch Book – Tony Bacon & Paul Day (Balafon)

Guitar Book – Tom Wheeler (Macdonald & Jane's)

Guitar Greats, The – John Tobler & Stuart Grundy (BBC Books)

Guitar Legends – Chris Gill (Studio Editions)

How The Fender Bass Changed The World – Jim Roberts (Backbeat Books)

Rock Guitarists Vol I (Guitar Player Books)

Rock Guitarists Vol II (Guitar Player Books)

Rock Hardware (Balafon)

Rockschool (BBC)

Seventeen Watts? – Mo Foster

(Sanctuary Publishing Ltd)

Stellas & Stratocasters – Willie G Moseley (Vintage Guitar Books)

What Bass? – Tony Bacon & Laurence Canty (Making Music)

Wired For Sound A Guitar Odyssey – Martin Melhuish & Mark Hall (Quarry Music Books)

Magazines: Guitar, Guitar Player, Total Guitar, Classic Rock, Guitarist